HOPE/NADĚJE

The Paintings of Jana Bemová

Claudia Zoeller and Joan Yesulaitis

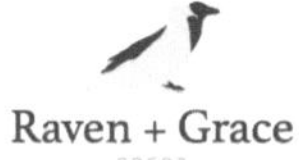

Raven + Grace
PRESS

Raven + Grace Press

Contents

Dedication

This book is dedicated to Jana's grandsons, Jenik Bem and Robert Zoeller.

Jana Bemova

Jana Bemová is a Czech painter whose life has spanned volatile periods of time from the Nazi occupation of Czechoslovakia to the communist takeover of the country and, finally, through the fall of the Soviet Union. She lived in exile in Europe and in the US for three decades, until her family's property was returned to her after democracy was re-established in the newly formed Czech Republic, now referred to as Czechia. Her paintings reflect the social struggles and emotional reflections of a woman moving between cultures, different political ideologies and locations, while raising her two daughters, at times, as a single mother.

Jana was born in Czechoslovakia in April 1940. Her earliest memories were a mixture of the sounds of sirens, warnings of incoming bombs, and the hourly bells that rang through the old city of Prague. Memories of time spent in the basement bomb shelter as a very small child contrasted with memories of the idyllic countryside in a shared multi-generational family home and long afternoons playing in the isolation of the surrounding greenery.

The Nazi occupation of Prague affected Jana's family directly. The family successfully protected the Jewish wife of their non-Jewish cousin by hiding her. However she was eventually taken to Terezin Concentration Camp outside of Prague, but fortunately she survived the war because she was able to work in the pharmacy of the camp.

After the war, Jana was primarily raised by her maternal grandmother. The family lived in an apartment/house on Trziste Street in the old city surrounding the castle. During the rule of the Habsburgs, which extended until the beginning of WWI, this area surrounding the castle housed many of the people who worked in the castle compound. Jana's grandfather bought the fifteenth-century house in 1918. Her family lost ownership of their property when the communists took over in 1948. They were eventually forced to move out of their home in Prague because it was considered too big for the number of people living there.

Jana struggled under communism as both an artist and as an exceptionally attractive young woman. When a high-ranking communist official began pressuring her to spy on some of her friends and report back to him on their activities, she knew it was time to flee Prague and communism. In 1968, after Soviet troops violently put down a political uprising with tanks rolling down the streets of Prague, she put her plan into action.

Jana was forced to leave Claudia, her preschool-aged daughter, with relatives and go to Paris alone. This was especially painful because she was a single mother. In Paris, she found other Czechs in exile. She studied art and worked odd jobs like passing out flyers in the French suburbs to survive. Finally, she was able to bring Claudia to Paris.

Prague Under Communism

Life under communist rule was very difficult. Although the family was officially allowed to keep ownership of their property, they were forced to move into a smaller apartment. Twelve meters were allowed for the kitchen space and twelve meters in the dwelling space per person. Jana's mother was allowed to manage the property, which had multiple apartments in it. However, she wasn't allowed to keep any of the rent money as this had to go to the government. Many families gave their properties to the communist government at this time instead of working for them. Luckily, Jana's family was able to reclaim ownership of their properties in the 1990s.

Jana's father, who had been trained as a lawyer, was forced to chop wood in the woods for two years as a logger. The communist government wanted him to know the experience of the working class. He was eventually allowed to work as a lawyer in an office with nine other lawyers. Jana's uncle, an industrious man and a former owner of a small lab that produced pharmaceuticals, was forced to work in a uranium mine.

Growing up under communism, Jana had to be careful at school. Saying the wrong thing could cause problems for the family. What an individual could achieve in society was limited. There was no incentive to work hard. People had to wait in line for meat, vegetables, and the basics of life. They had to search and barter for goods. There was a lot of corruption and the system divided people in ways that they had to keep hidden. At parties, no one could say what they really thought because anyone could be a spy. Many competent people who didn't support the government were not allowed to work and their children were not allowed to study. The communist government pressured many people to spy for them under the threat of persecution.

Everyone in society had to work. People who didn't work were called "Prizivnik", a derogatory term meaning someone who takes without giving anything back. Jana had to join a society of artists that did work sanctioned by the government. She designed book covers for textbooks to be used in the communist schools.

The portfolio Jana created while working in this job actually helped her get a prestigious job in the Western world many years later. After the Soviet troops invaded Czechoslovakia in 1968, she realized that she needed to get out of Prague. There were mass protests against these forces leading to greater pressure to keep the citizens under control. A few years earlier, in 1965, communists tried to force Jana to work for them as a spy to get information on her friends and colleagues. She was able to put the communist officials off by pretending to be unintelligent. In 1968 Jana was already studying art in Paris. It wasn't difficult to get out of Czechoslovakia on her student visa.

She had to prepare before leaving communist Prague permanently because her daughter, Claudia, was three-and-a-half at the time. Jana decided to go to Paris first on her own. She knew nothing about living in the Western world. She studied art in Paris and connected with many of the Czechoslovakian refugees there—many of whom had moved to Paris from Czechoslovakia in 1948, and again in 1968, in two giant waves of migration.

Jana knew that the connections she made with these refugees in Paris would help her find a job, which was especially important since she had a small child she was raising on her own.

She brought Claudia to Paris where they lived in a small house. The Czech refugee community helped her, along with French people from the left side of politics. On one occasion, the French police called Jana into the station and interviewed her for three hours under the accusation that she was a Czech spy. The year 1968 was a period of social tension in Paris with lots of student protests and riots instigated by left wing politics. Many of her artist friends held these same beliefs. She convinced the French police that she wasn't a spy or any threat to French society.

She studied art and delivered paper advertisements in the Parisian suburbs for extra money. This led to her fear of dogs, which is sometimes depicted in her paintings. Although there were fences in front of the properties, the dogs barked viciously when anyone approached. The dogs in Jana's paintings reflect not only this fear but also the atmosphere at that time. The dogs are like a "mood ring", showing whether the painting is happy or not, according to their expression.

Jana had been accepted to study engraving at L'Ecole de Beaux Arts, but her utensils disappeared regularly. It was difficult to be a beautiful, blond refugee who barely spoke French. Instead of going to class, she got special permission to go to the Louvre every day and copied Botticelli's "Madonna and Child". She was in Paris without Claudia at that time. Jana's fixation on this painting reflected how deeply she missed her young daughter. In the fall of 1968 she was able to bring Claudia back with her to Paris after a brief trip back to Prague.

It was difficult to make money in Paris with a child, so Jana decided to go to the US with Claudia. While pregnant, she broke up with Claudia's father who was a traveling musician from California. His family had rejected Jana because they thought she was a communist. She was determined to go to the US and get citizenship on her own and finally received a visa to go to New York. There was a problem with the airplane, and all the passengers were held in the airport until it was fixed. The passengers all got sick from the food they were fed by the airline. It was an inauspicious arrival into the US. She stayed with friends and found help settling in until she could find a place of her own.

She obtained a job at Macmillan Publishers designing children's textbooks and worked there for eight years. She sketched and designed the layout of the textbooks, following the process all the way through to the printing. Jana soon became the art director and design manager in the textbook department. She worked with famous illustrators and photographers to illustrate the textbooks (and Claudia was actually in some of the textbooks). It was a very hectic and pressure-filled job. For Claudia, as a child in class, it was an awkward experience when her picture was sometimes part of the daily lesson.

In 1979, Jana decided to marry her Czech boyfriend, Honza Bem, and move to Florida. She was able to stop working at the publishing company and had time to paint and focus on doing her artwork. Jana's second daughter, Jan Marie, was born a few years later when Claudia was sixteen. The sequence of paintings represented in this book span the time of Jana's escape from communism and her transition into life in the Western world.

Architectural Paintings

The streets, winding staircases, and archways of Prague appear throughout Jana's work. At times, a literal representation transforming into a surrealistic dreamscape that mixes time and space, Prague is part of the metaphorical, internal imagery recurring in her works.

Hope

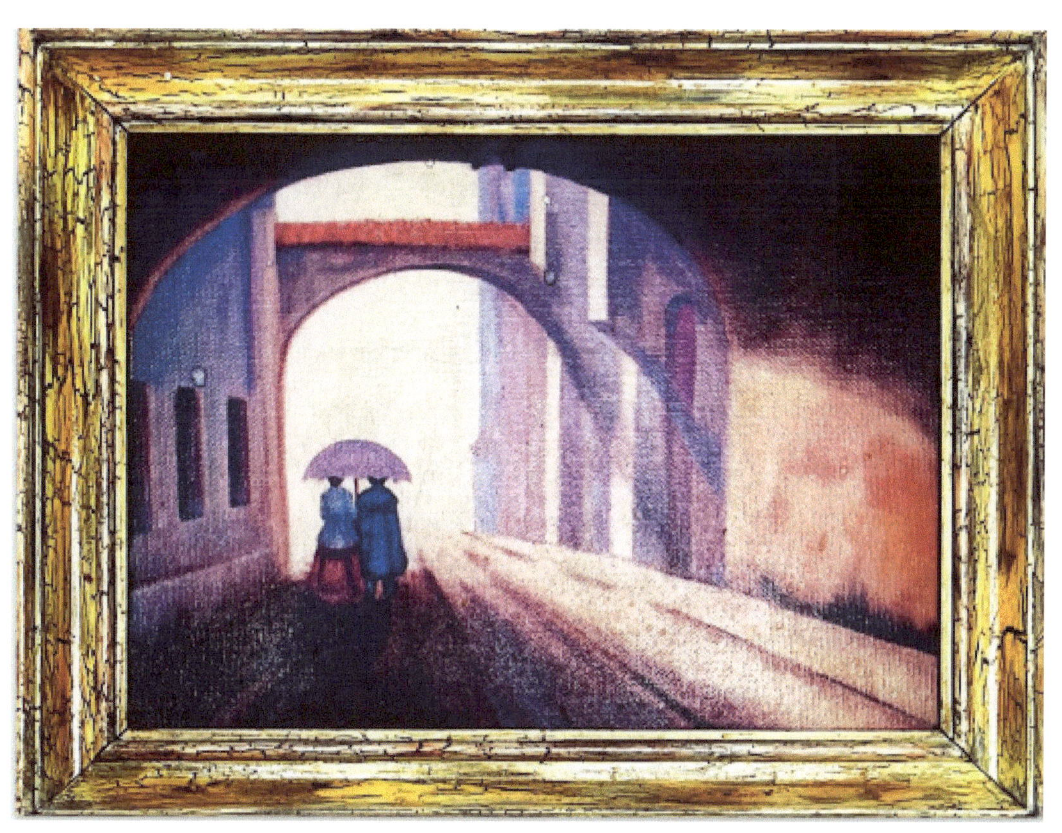

This architectural painting shows two women with an umbrella, Jana and Claudia, strolling towards the sunshine at the end of a typical Prague archway. They have been life companions on their journey out of communistic Prague to the West and back again after the fall of communism.

Jana, barely able to speak French or English, left her family's conservative, controlling Czech lifestyle under communism to go to an unknown world in the democratic West. The transition was harsh and fraught with difficulties, but she couldn't bear to have her daughter grow up in such a restricted environment. She also yearned for artistic freedom that was only possible somewhere else.

The darkness of repression is behind the two women. The optimistic light in front of them is accessible at the end of the ancient archway. The kind of future that awaited the two women beyond the traditional arches and lifestyle of Prague was impossible to know at the time of their escape. Very little information was available in the late 1960s to citizens from behind the Iron Curtain of the Soviet Bloc countries as to actual circumstances of what a new life in the West would be like for them.

The future was full of hopeful aspirations for someone like Jana who was willing to work hard. By contrast, communism provided the Czech people with the basics for survival and didn't encourage a strong work ethic towards a certain goal. Citizens were only cogs in a large governmental system with no room for individuality. The women are leaving the stability of their traditional life behind. In sharing the same umbrella, they share the same dream, working together harmoniously to move forward. They have each other as they move from a known, secure, and structured world into an unknown, insecure and unstructured world.

The two women are united against hardships and obstacles that will be encountered in the new world outside of the familiar arches of Prague. As single mother for most of Claudia's early childhood, living alone in Paris and New York, Jana and her daughter had no other familial support system. The closeness of their bond instinctually, physically, and spiritually is seen as the two women hold onto each other underneath a shared umbrella. Their souls are commingled and motivated by their shared desire to survive and thrive in their new chosen life, moving forward together as one.

This painting reflects many of the themes developed throughout Jana's paintings. The strong mother-daughter bond, a focus on the female experience, escape from communistic Prague into the unknown West, and a sense of hope by moving from darkness into light are all explored in Jana's work. These two women were and are everything to each other. Their strength, courage, and determination are simply and powerfully depicted in this painting, aptly titled "Hope".

Charles Bridge

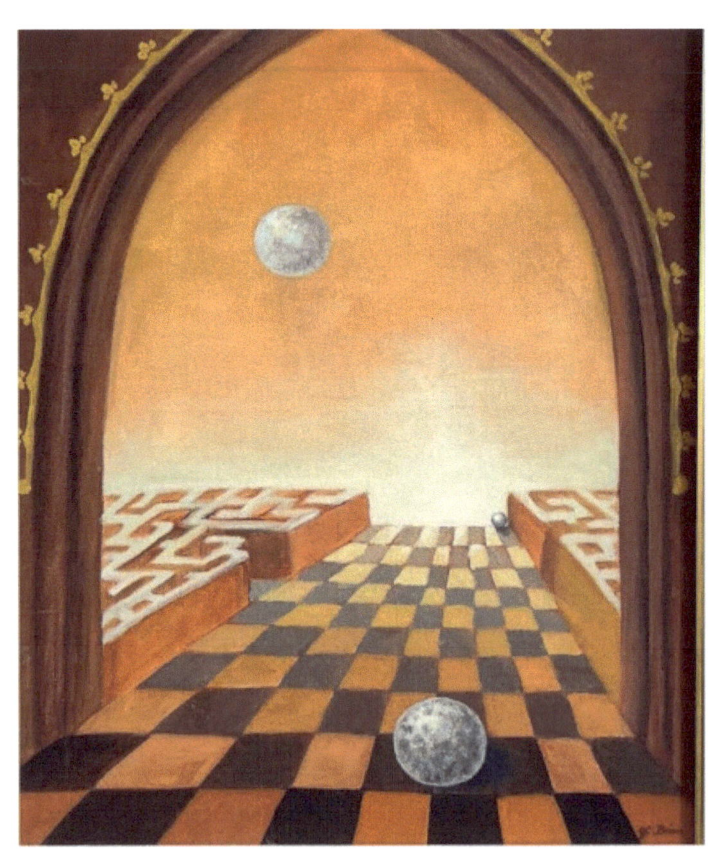

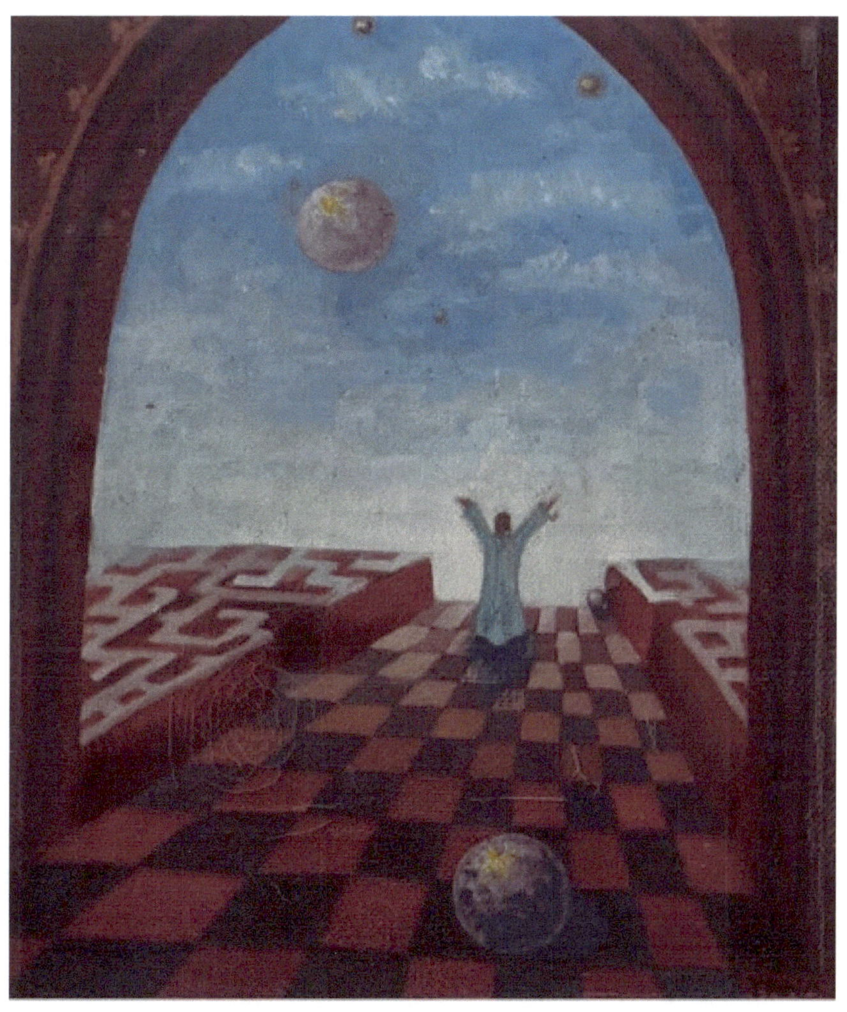

In September 1890, the Great Flood knocked down a portion of the Charles Bridge in Prague. At that time, wooden rafts were used to transport objects on the river. The many large wooden rafts on the river during the flood were pushed together with floating logs, breaking off two large sections of the Charles Bridge and causing the collapse of two arches. Jana's grandmother recounted this story so many times that this scenario frequently appeared in Jana's dreams. In her dream, she is walking on Charles Bridge when suddenly the bridge disappears from under her feet.

There are two paintings in this series. The original painting doesn't have a figure. In the second painting, Jana painted over a copy of the first painting. She added a figure at the end looking over the abyss and a sunrise, as if light and hope were on the horizon, turning something frightening into something redemptive.

The position of the first dark ball in the middle of the checkerboard floor pattern underneath the arch is an obstacle, weighing the viewer down. The pathway leads into the unknown. Beyond the checkerboard floor, floating in the sphere of the unknown is another moon-like ball representing hope and leaving the obstacles behind. The moon floating in the sky represents movement into a new dimension of hope and expansion, no longer limited, controlled, or dragged behind. This is an undiscovered starting point for new life energy to emerge and develop. This painting reflects a common theme present in much of Jana's work. There is emotional darkness in the front, moving into the light from a restricted, predictable, and regimented environment into freedom. The maze represents the controlled environment that entraps without a clear way through to an uncertain end. This represents endless obstacles and confusing pathways in a restrictive society. This painting represents moving out of fear, taking risks, and finding a new expansiveness in life.

There is a regal nature in the architectural elements of this painting. Jana's family had been part of the bourgeoisie in Czech society. Even within the difficulties and restrictions of communism, her family had more material possessions than many others. The arches represent the gilded prison from which Jana had to free herself. The ball that is on the checked floor is trapped, while the ball in the sky is free. The architectural elements are very typical of Prague. This is what Jana left behind to jump into an unknown space without any personal or family ties, but an empty sky full of possibility.

The second painting in this series was a color print that Jana painted over. Red predominates, which represents strength, but also pain, blood, and difficulty. The rock on the ground is hard but has a golden sheen. The small figure at the edge of the abyss is raising her hands victoriously and confidently. She isn't afraid and has many new worlds of opportunity, represented by the planets floating in the hopeful blue sky above. The dark red at the front of the painting represents pain and suffering, which is transformed into hopeful optimism in the blue sky. Jana returned to this painting years after the first "Charles Bridge" painting when the family finally had their property returned to them after the fall of communism in the Velvet Revolution.

The 2 Blue Ladies

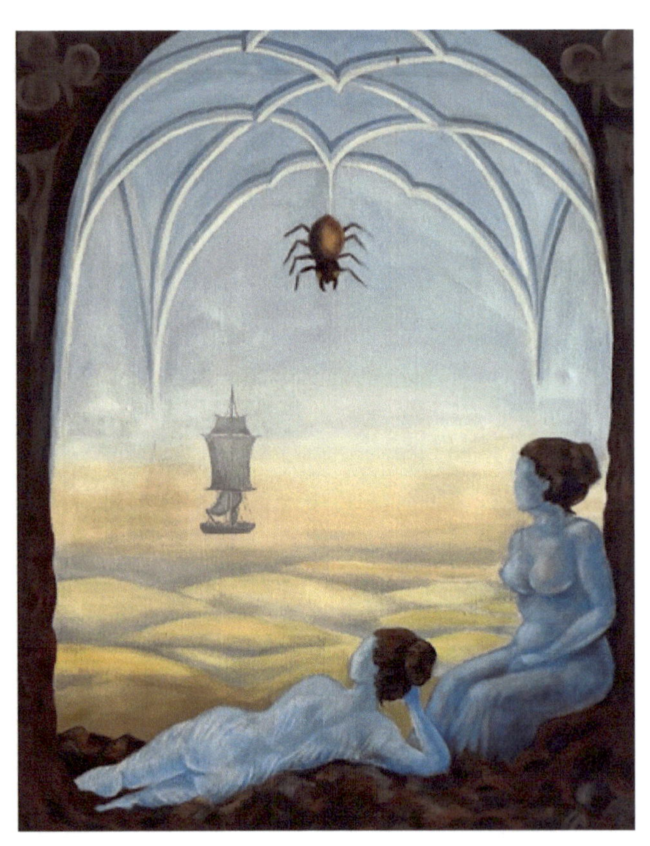

This painting depicts two nude women with blue skin under an archway gazing out into the distance at a boat on the water. The women long to be somewhere else. These women are very comfortable with themselves, and their bodies are trapped in a situation. The material underneath them is like quicksand, trapping the women in the earth below. They yearn for the light and hope in the distance but are unable to move beyond the spider hanging from the arch. For the women to escape to their promising future, they must get beyond the spider and its elaborate crystal web.

The ocean, with its unpredictable waves and strong currents, represents freedom and the possibility of taking the women into another realm of hope in life. The water close to them is very turbulent, but becomes calmer further in the distance. The boat could take the women to a place where they could be unconstrained and liberated. The spider keeps them trapped.

The spider with its crystal web is a gatekeeper, representing the social and personal forces that are obstacles to these women's freedom. The crystal web is ornate and reminiscent of the arches of a cathedral. The spiderweb, like hanging ice crystals, emits a chill. The two women are cold and isolated, away from the warmth of the water beyond the arches. The ornate arches represent social pressures and traditional expectations that control and limit the women's freedom. The menacing spider has fangs and represents fear that must be overcome to move forward. The frozen spiderweb is a complicated series of difficult tasks to be maneuvered.

The theme of escaping into an uncertain future from a safe but constrictive environment repeats throughout Jana's paintings. It reflects the reality of her life under communism. Although life was controlled by a repressive social system and government, there weren't concerns about paying the bills. The government took care of its citizens and gave a sense of security despite the social restrictions. Many citizens tolerated the restrictive environment because it gave them basic survival, but Jana could not.

The "2 Blue Ladies" depicts a period of preparation. A time of waiting for the right moment to move forward into a hopeful new realm. Life under communism had to be carefully considered. Citizens living under restrictions could see where they wanted to go but had to plan every detail and wait for the right time to act. Usually, the back of the painting, which shows depth, is blue. In this case, the colors are reversed.

The blue women aren't joyful, like the sunshine over the water through the arch. They are frozen, pondering their situation, hoping to move into the warmth of life and the blue skies above.

Jana had to plan out most aspects of her early life. Her escape from Prague with Claudia was the most daunting. Claudia was Jana's only companion for many years before her marriage. The seated woman represents the mother with her arms in a position of restraint. The reclining woman is her daughter, who is open and not constrained by an adult understanding of the conditions around her. This painting recalls planning their escape from the beautiful but restrictive arches of Prague under communism into the uncertain but unrestricted future overseas that was yet to come.

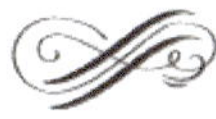

The Courtyard Stroll in Autumn

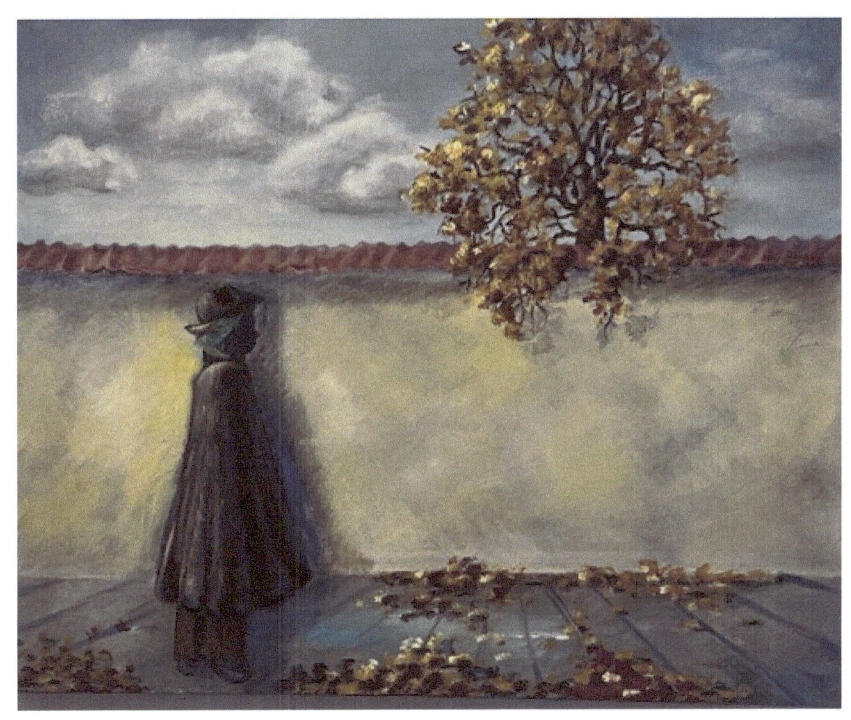

The scene depicted in the painting is reminiscent of a typical wall in Prague. The painting is paradoxical, with both bright and shadowy tones. The woman in a trench coat trudging down the cobblestones seems both lost and at odds with where she is while looking out into what could be possible, trying to find balance. This woman has a solitary relationship with life, even if surrounded by others. The people and circumstances around her don't connect with her true nature.

The tree represents life and hope. The blue sky represents freedom. The leaves on the ground represent loss, confusion, and death, which will be left behind as she continues her stroll.

The woman strolls beneath the wall where there is no life and vitality. It's autumn, and the leaves are falling off the trees, with winter just around the corner. As time goes by, the woman feels older and blocked off from the flow of life at this moment. But her stroll will continue, hopefully beyond this cycle of nature with its endings and decay. Although there is a sadness and feeling of gloomy introspection represented by the deep purple, the vitality of the green shows a certainty that spring will come after winter when the cycle of life renews.

Roles of Women in Communist Prague

Living under communist limitations was unacceptable for Jana, especially as the young, single mother of a small child. Although she was able to escape to the Western, democratic world, the limiting social roles for women from her past shaped her early life. These paintings reflect choices and outcomes under those limiting conditions. The sequence of these paintings depict the life of a woman from adolescence, through adulthood, and middle age. It's as if Jana was imagining how her life would have been if she had stayed in Prague.

The Card Game

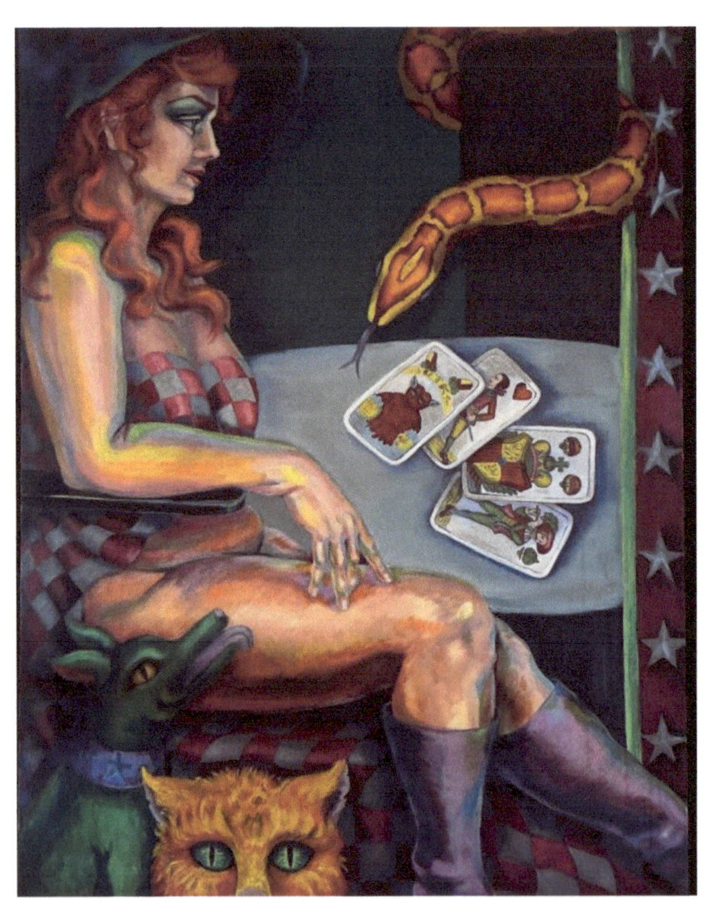

The beautiful, young, red-haired woman is at the beginning of her life. The old-fashioned purple hat shows her high social status. The red head is a young femme fatale at the peak of her youthful beauty, poised to pick a life partner. She is contemplating this fateful decision that will affect the trajectory of her life. The voluptuous woman's negligee is the pattern of a checkerboard, reflecting all the possible moves and choices to be made and their consequences. Her boots protect the woman and ground her. The poll with the stars is an optimistic goal post reflecting a victorious happy future, but the snake wrapped around it denotes danger and misfortune if the wrong partner is chosen. The snake evokes a feeling of Eve, before the fall, listening to the snake wrapped around the forbidden tree. The young woman is at a turning point of moving from the innocence and freedom of youth into the binding responsibility of adulthood.

The cards on the table are her potential partners. The devil card is a destructive, controlling relationship with a man. The woman is afraid of the devil, but he can offer financial stability. The second man with the heart card, her ideal lover, is loving, protective, and strong. He is someone the woman wishes she could be with. The third card represents the social pressure and judgment that affect the young woman's decision. The last card represents a financially stable, nature-oriented partner who inspires freedom and creativity.

But the devil card in the front is dominating and blocking all the other possibilities. The young woman can never be completely free or creative because the devil card's energy is in a position of power over all the other cards and choices in the card game. Relationships are the luck of the draw, like this card game.

The green dog by the woman's side is a protective pet bound by its beautiful purple collar, the same color as the young woman's hat. The dog is well taken care of but controlled by its master, reflective of the role the woman could play, depending on the choice she makes. The cat's green eyes peer out, knowingly, representing the young woman's instinctual knowledge of the situation she finds herself in.

The young woman in the painting has a limited number of options to choose from depending on the cards she was dealt. There were only certain options available to her, reflective of the social pressures in the period Jana grew up in. The woman, like Jana, must make hard choices to survive.

Czech Cultural Connections

Czech people frequently play cards. The cards in "The Card Game" are from the traditional Czech Mariasch card game, one of the most popular card games in the Czech Republic. It is part of the King-Queen family of Ace to Ten games with a simplified scoring system. This creative deck of cards, often played in Czech pubs, involves matching cards with the same suits together.

Personal Connections

Jana is mortified by snakes and frequently paints her fears. This large yellow snake looks particularly venomous. She assimilates and transforms what she's afraid of by painting it. The young red-haired woman's lack of fear is an ideal that Jana seeks to embody in her own life.

Motifs

Hats repeatedly appear in Jana's paintings. They reflect the subject's attitude and social position. Hats are popular and worn frequently by Czech women.

Boots also appear frequently. They are protective and grounding. Jana often didn't feel safe in her surroundings. The boots seem to say, "be careful where you tread."

Jana stylizes dogs and cats, often combining them into imaginary creatures. These animals archetypically reflect social roles, her feelings or mood, and/or the level of danger in the world around her.

The Soldier

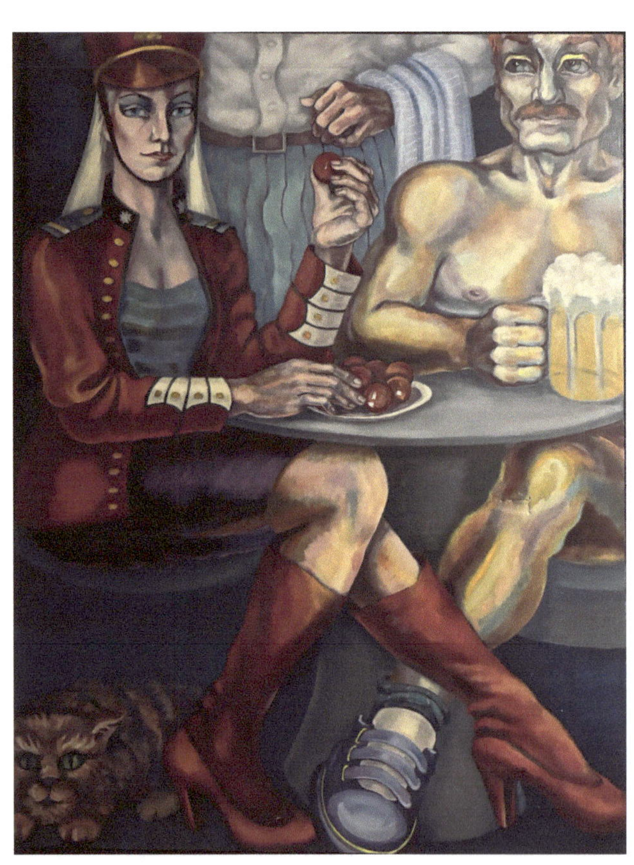

In "The Soldier", red, the color of communism, represents strict governmental and social control. A beautiful blond woman is depicted in an obviously communist red uniform, sitting at a table. A sexy blue camisole peaks out from the opened uniformed jacket along with a tight purple skirt and red high-heeled boots. The beautiful soldier has striking makeup and perfectly coiffed straight blond hair. She has adapted to what the official communist society expects her to be.

The faceless man behind her with a cloth over his arm seems to be a waiter, but the woman is giving him a piece of her red fruit from the table. The man's hands are dark and dirty, suggesting corruption.

She must give back to the patriarchal state a large portion of whatever fruits her labor produces. The waiter's formal striped pants are like restrictive bars in a jail cell, hovering around the woman, keeping her in line. His bulging pelvis suggests the dominant male sexualized energy that controls the woman. Although she must feed him with her red plums, the woman herself is also like an exotic treat to be consumed and enjoyed. Her empty stare projects the unhappy acceptance of the role she is forced to play.

The green-eyed cat hiding quietly under the woman's seat is trapped, not daring to make a move. It sees everything going on around it but is powerless. Similarly, the woman must hide her true nature. Her natural instincts and impulses are hidden and controlled by the red uniform and the social expectations around her. Like the cowering cat, she must powerlessly accept circumstances as they are.

By contrast, the shirtless man next to the soldier is earthy and sensual. He doesn't have an official uniform or position and is content to sit at the table drinking a pint of frothy beer. The shirtless man doesn't have to play a particular role, the same way the woman does. The woman's red boots are beautiful, but uncomfortable and binding. The shirtless man's sneakers have Velcro ties that slip on and off easily. The man is living and expressing his carnal nature, unrestricted in this way in society, unlike the woman. The man doesn't have to hide his true nature to serve the state. His glassy, empty stare looks past the woman. She's there, but her circumstances and limitations don't interest him in his inebriation.

This painting accurately depicts the party lifestyle and how many Czechs coped with living in such a restrictive communist state. The woman put on her uniform and played her prescribed role during the day. After hours, there was drinking and partying to alleviate the constraints of living with repression. Some men, in positions of power, got their hands dirty demanding favors, feeding off powerless, controlled women. Other men drank themselves into oblivion, anesthetized to the plight of those around them. The woman in the red soldier uniform must balance between these two kinds of men while hiding her true nature to survive.

The Elegant Woman

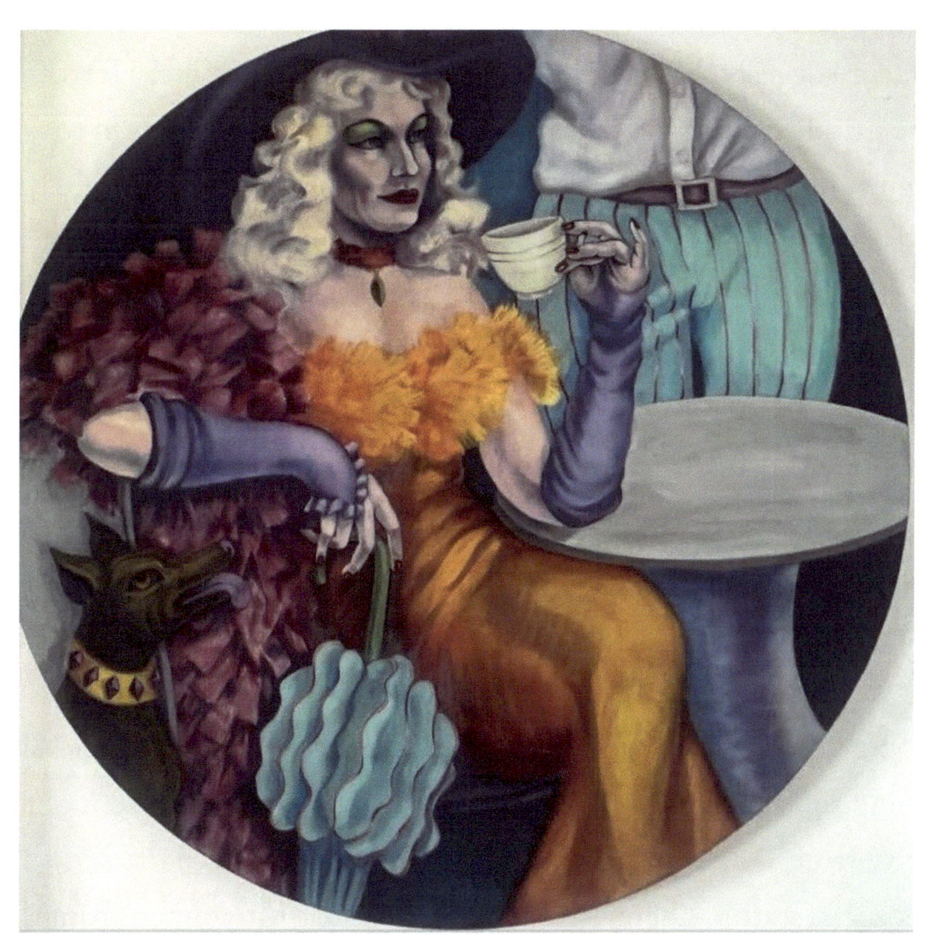

This elegant woman emits the desire to fit in with society. She is alluring and comfortably sensual in a reserved way. Image is important to the elegant woman as she casually sips coffee in a dramatic hat with a coquettish umbrella at her side. She's middle aged but still attractive, with heavy makeup covering the lines in her face. The makeup is a painted-on mask showing the world what it wants to see in her. Her flowing dress and matching shawl exude style and femininity. The bright colors attract wanted attention.

The colors orange and red reflect that her energy in life is centered on survival and sensuality. The orange dress shows that her sensuality is the dominant force in her life. The red shawl, loosely around her shoulders, suggests that she isn't grounded or secure in life. Her security comes from her sensuality. The purple gloves show that traditional norms and beliefs in society also limit her, binding her arms and choices. "The Elegant Woman" expresses herself well and has all the required social graces. Her face is painted into the perfect expression of grace and style.

The dog by her side is green, an archetypal symbol reflecting the woman's soul. It is controlled by a yellow collar with violet stones. The sharply cut violet stones represent traditional values. The dog's collar mirrors the elegant woman's red choker with a green stone. The dog is a beautiful but controlled pet, unable to express its true nature and to freely love. The elegant woman is a beautiful and controlled creature in much the same way. Her red choker represents the need for security that controls her choices. The small, green, dagger-like stone pointed towards her heart shows that the elegant woman does love the man who controls her, but it's at a cost. She can't love freely and naturally.

The elegant women's eyes betray the difficulties she has endured in life. She smiles for the world while covering up the painful past. "The Elegant Woman" also represents the ideal kind of Czech femininity from Jana's upbringing. Despite communism, Jana came from a bourgeois family with higher social status. There was immense pressure for women from this social stratum to conform by projecting a certain acceptable image. "The Elegant Woman" embodies this ideal to perfection. Projecting the correct image was a means of entry into certain worlds. Women were both permitted and prohibited from getting into certain desirable places based on projecting the correct image of wealth in communist Prague.

Under communism in the Czech Republic, there were two different kinds of currency. Only certain people could get the kind of currency needed to shop in certain higher-end stores. Tuzex was a store that sold better quality meat, food items, and home goods to the higher social stratum. The elegant woman would have had access to this kind of store, while someone wearing jeans and a T-shirt would not be allowed in.

The professionally dressed but faceless man behind the woman is depicted with his lower torso only, showing the male-dominated core of society during communism. There are always these kinds of powerful men in nice suits hanging around. The elegant woman has power because of the beauty that enables her to move through a society dominated by male energy. Beauty is her social power. Society under communism was male dominated with limiting, traditional social roles for women. The man's pinstriped pants are like prison bars, obstructing the woman's view and potentially controlling her movement. The man's face is not important enough to be shown because these kinds of men are all the same. Dressing the part attracts this kind of man, and that is the elegant woman's motivation in life to survive.

The elegant woman is very satisfying to men, but she isn't making a real emotional connection to them. To survive, she gives them what they want. This is a role she has been allowed to play throughout her life, and her last relationship of this kind has ended. She's still attractive and young enough to play the game. Once again, it has worked.

Struggle/ Identity

Jana was fulfilled in her role as a mother. After losing her own mother, Jana's maternal grandmother was the foundational parental figure in her life. This series of paintings explores Jana's feelings as a mother and as a daughter and expresses a sense of independent identity and self-understanding.

The Discussion

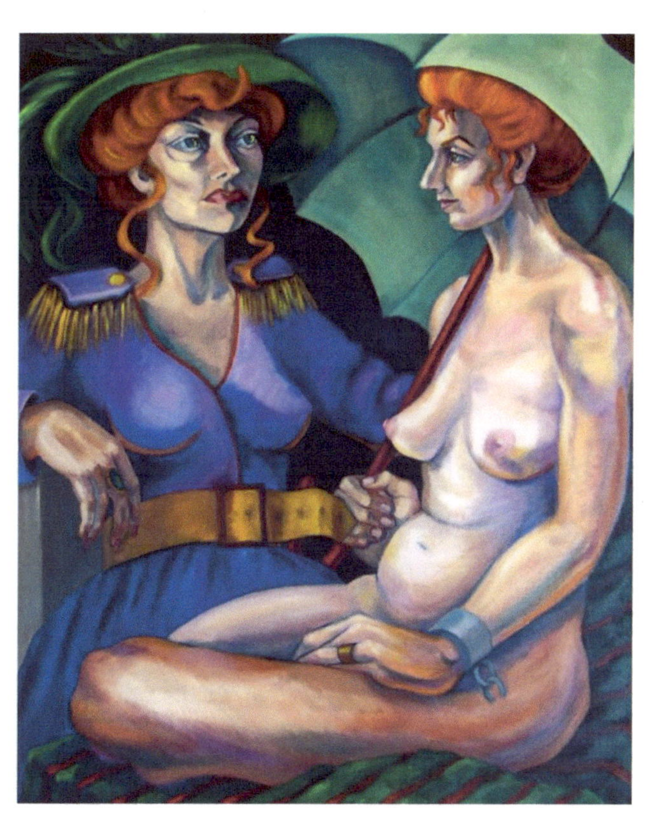

The strong-willed middle-aged woman on the left, dressed in regal purple with yellow military trim, is in sharp contrast to the young nude woman on the right. The purple dress represents traditional values and morality. The yellow belt and military shoulder pads show the middle-aged woman's strength and control, imposing her beliefs and ideals on the younger woman.

The younger, nude woman doesn't have the traditional beliefs or limitations of the older woman. She is comfortable with herself and her body. Although her gaze is softer, she doesn't comply with the older woman's opinion on how to live. Her right hand is clenched in a fist, showing defiance. The younger woman is wearing a shackle with a broken chain on her left hand, having broken free of the antiquated limitations that the older woman still lives by and espouses.

Both women have fiery red hair, which shows a familial connection. The older woman's deep green hat is traditional and formal. The younger woman's lighter green hat is softer and more organic looking. Although these two women are clearly at odds with each other, they are surrounded by the green energy of love that binds them together. Their opposition and discussions continue, with the younger woman refusing to deny her true nature and the older woman holding onto her rigid, traditional beliefs.

The young nude woman represents Jana in spirit. Influenced by the hippie movement of the 1960s, she often clashed with her more traditional grandmother who was born in 1882 and a product of the repressed Victorian era. She was always perfectly dressed and had impeccable manners. Jana's grandmother commanded the family, like a general, reflective in the regal purple dress with yellow military trim.

The broken shackle on the younger woman's wrist represents Jana breaking free from these outdated beliefs while also alluding to her eventual escape from communist-controlled Prague to a new life in the free world.

The Green Dog

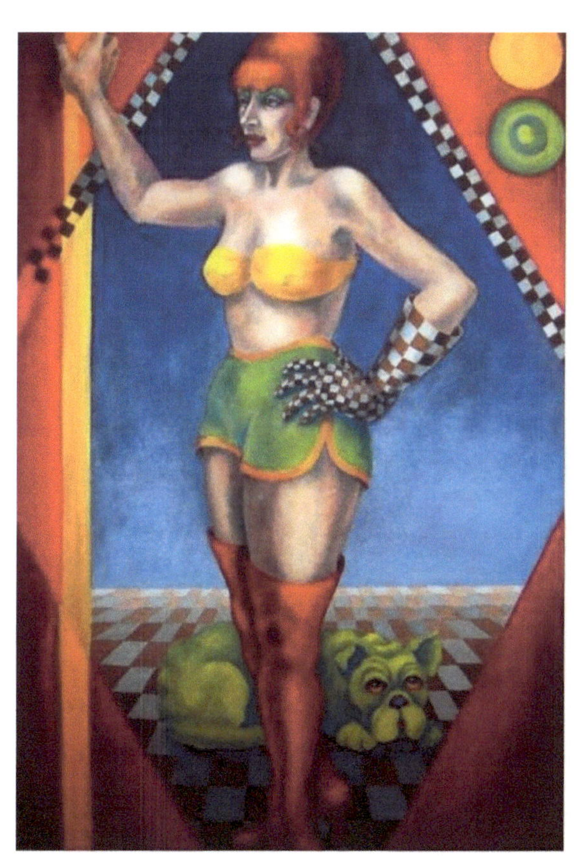

The red-headed woman standing in an entryway is moving into an unknown realm, full of uncertainty. The woman is finding the strength to move forward after making difficult decisions. The woman's upper body, representing her feminine exterior, is flashy and toned in a yellow bikini top. Her shorts are sporty and athletic, a typical outfit for warm, tropical weather.

In contrast, her red thigh-high boots are more sleek and sophisticated winter gear. The extra-long boots are protective and grounding. Her gloved left hand and forearm reflect the pattern in the curtain and on the floor. The checkered pattern on her arm, the curtains and the floor reflect all the strategic moves that the woman had to make to get to this transition.

The woman is paused on the threshold of a new situation. The red on the walls are her previous circumstances. She appears reticent and reflective. Like traffic lights signaling stop, caution, and go, she has conflicting feelings and fear about taking this step forward. The world behind her is like the night sky. The sun has set on the past, which was happy and secure.

The green dog cowering behind the woman peers out with frightened yellow eyes. The dog represents the woman's instinctual fear, despite her strong appearance. The dog also depicts a frightened, dependent child, clinging to its current circumstances, unhappy and unwilling to make a change.

The woman is determined to move through the threshold and into a new experience. Her fiery red hair mirroring her fiery red boots reflect her determination. She will bring her head and feet together, stepping into a new, unknown world. The unfinished corner represents her unfinished story and the uncertainty of how things will unfold.

Jana painted this portrait as she was transitioning from New York City to Miami. The woman's clothing is for tropical Miami weather while the boots and glove are for much cooler New York City. Like the painted woman's clothing, Jana was emotionally partially in both places, letting go of the winter-wear for more tropical garb—both literally and emotionally.

Jana's painting style and use of color changed after this transition. She worried about young Claudia, a deeply sensitive child, and how she would adapt to her new life. Their shared experience of leaving New York City and moving to the completely different environment of Miami was a frightening and uncertain new beginning, as reflected in this painting.

The Green Cat

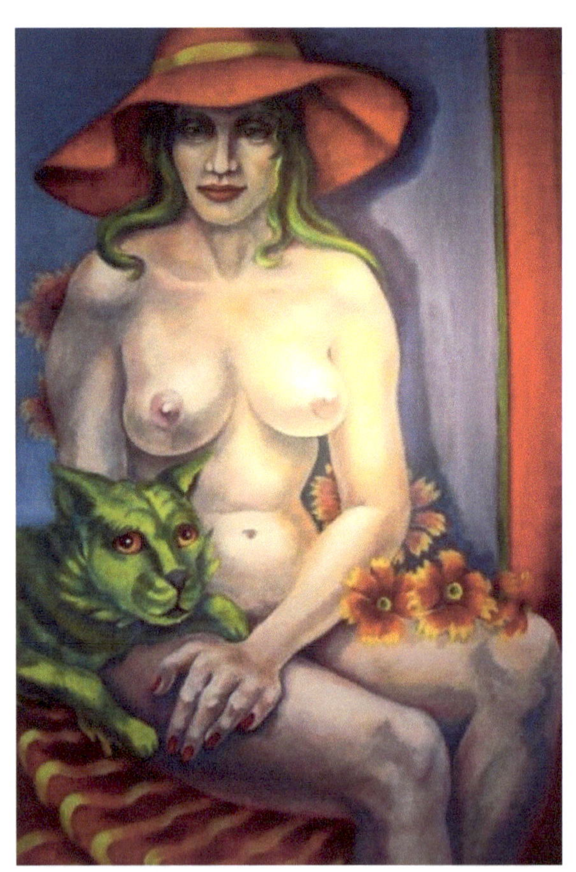

The nude woman portrayed is comfortable with her body and instinctual nature. She is nurturing a fictional dog/cat creature. These imaginary creatures often appear in Jana's paintings and represent different instinctual impulses. Although there is a slight resemblance to a dog that Jana had, in this case it represents a person, most likely a child, who is clinging to the woman for strength. The creature's intense red eyes represent a knowingness, despite its timidity. The cat-dog has had difficulties in life and though co-dependently attached to the woman, needs to find its own strength.

Hats are a motif in Jana's work, used to show a person's role or social status. This red sun hat with a yellow ribbon represents grounding and control. The woman's green hair, the same color as the creature's fur, shows their familial connection. The red, yellow, and orange flowers next to the woman show her fulfillment in nurturing the creature. The striped blanket underneath the woman and creature, the same colors as the flowers, represents the structure the woman is creating to soothe the animal.

The act of nurturing the creature is spiritually fulfilling, as shown in the violet background. This woman embodies a powerful maternal nature. Being a mother and caring for the needy, frightened creature attached to her comes naturally to the woman. Grounding and nurturing, the green cat-dog nurtures, grounds, and fulfills the woman. Motherhood, a role she chose for herself at an early age, was always vital to Jana's personal fulfillment. The loving energy of motherhood is the central theme of this painting.

Portraits and Reflections on Love

The two complementary portraits are of Jana and Claudia with both paintings set on different sides of a fictional landscape.

The last two paintings reflect aspects of romantic love in dreamy surreal landscapes.

Woman Floating on a Cloud Looking Down at the World

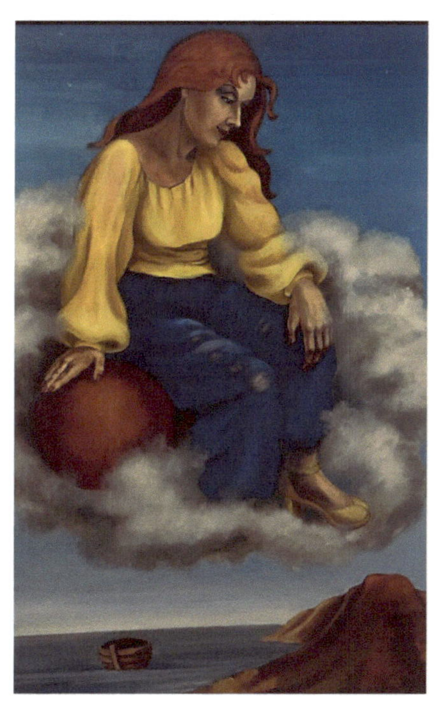

The red-haired woman is floating on a smoky cloud above a desolate, volcanic landscape next to a still body of water. A single empty boat is anchored off the shore. She is detached, contemplating the barren world below from a safe distance, avoiding any possible lava that could explode unexpectedly. The rocky, arid land is lonely and uninviting.

The cloud, an enjoyable, secure space, is a contrast to the empty, stagnant landscape stretching along the deep blue sea. The red-haired woman is nurtured by something beyond what she can find on earth. She is seated on a giant red ball, which stabilizes and grounds her. The red-haired woman doesn't feel completely part of this world. The yellow shirt reflects her self-control and self-motivation. The indigo harem pants represent the inspiration and visions that are part of a painter's daily life.

Clouds evoke the bright, joyful memories of airplane travel, which was a large part of Jana, Claudia, and their family's life. Whether flying back and forth from Miami to Prague, through the Czech countryside, or around the world, clouds were visible through so many airplane windows. Claudia's childhood dream was to escape and live in one of the bright, happy clouds floating by. There is always sun above the clouds, no matter how dreary a rainy day is below. Clouds signify hope and movement above the empty stagnation below.

Jana often paints women with red hair at times in her life when she needs to find strength. The barren landscape below signifies a time in life that is stagnant and not fulfilling. The red-haired woman finds fulfillment in detaching from the emptiness of the world and observing the landscape from afar in a world of her own making. She grounds herself by taking control of her life and creativity, as reflected in the yellow blouse, and focusing on her inner visions, as shown in her indigo pants. Despite the stagnation of the barren landscape below, there is movement in the blue sky and in the water. Blue is the color of expression.

The red-haired woman floating on a cloud represents the artistic process and lifestyle that fulfills Jana. Artistic detachment and observation of the sometimes barren, stagnant, and unfulfilling world around her is a coping mechanism for her. She creates her own world through the artistic process which is self-fulfilling and not dependent on attachment to the outside world.

The Claudia Painting

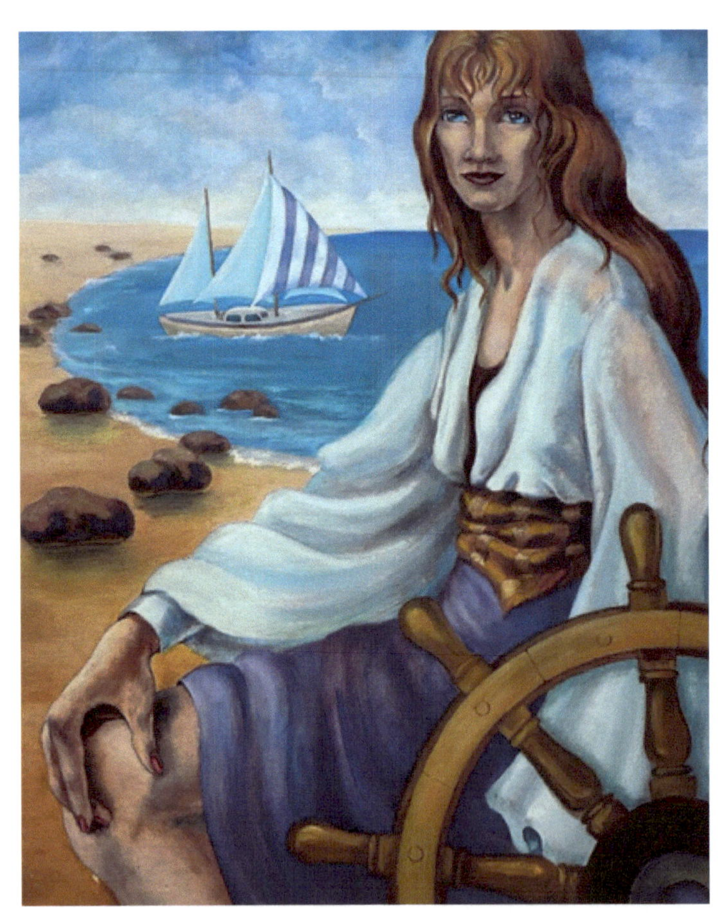

This portrait of Claudia depicts a young woman by the water. Water has always been a part of Claudia and Jana's life. When they lived in New York, they visited Long Island on the weekends, spending lots of time by the water. This imaginary landscape that is behind the young woman evokes a feeling of solitude, of being an individual on a singular path, not influenced by outside forces. The steering wheel of the ship in front of her shows her ability to move her life in the direction she wants to follow. This is in stark contrast to the social forces that controlled and steered her mother's life.

Although in this youthful depiction of Claudia, she isn't sure of exactly where she wants to go. The horizon is open. As a young woman, she needs to learn how to steer her own life forward, instead of being steered by the people around her. No one is steering for her, but she is content to stay where she is at this moment of possibility and open horizons.

The rock obstacles in her path on the beach aren't so daunting. Claudia will be able to go where she wants to go when she figures out where that is. Full of promise and possibility at this age, she hasn't left port to embark on whatever adventures life has to offer.

The young woman embodies strength and a natural ease within herself and in nature. She is someone who can and will move around the world at the right moment. The young Claudia will move beyond any obstacles to get on a ship to go to a better place. Movement and adventure are integral to her character. In this companion painting to "The Floating Woman" (a self-portrait of Jana as an artist), Claudia is a positive, hopeful person bringing the sunshine, finding a way over the obstacles, and moving into brighter horizons.

The young woman is grounded in the earth. Her blue eyes, as reflected in the deep blue water behind her, represent her empathy and spiritual connection to nature. Her strength and natural instincts help young Claudia navigate around and over obstacles and into more pleasant shores.

The landscape her mother is floating over in the companion painting is more desolate and less hopeful.

It's as if the two paintings form one landscape with the floating Jana looking down on her young, beautiful daughter, Claudia, and all the optimistic energy she embodies. The floating woman isn't anchored to the earth; she's a creature from another realm. While the young woman is an extension of the landscape, grounded and vital. When the time is right, she will figure out a way over the rocks and onto the ship to get to a better place.

This is a portrait of a youthful, natural woman who finds ways to solve problems and help move life forward for herself and for her mother. There will always be another ship after a rocky path that the young woman will find her way to. Her instincts, evolved and pure, combined with the best intentions help her to find the way.

Soul Mates

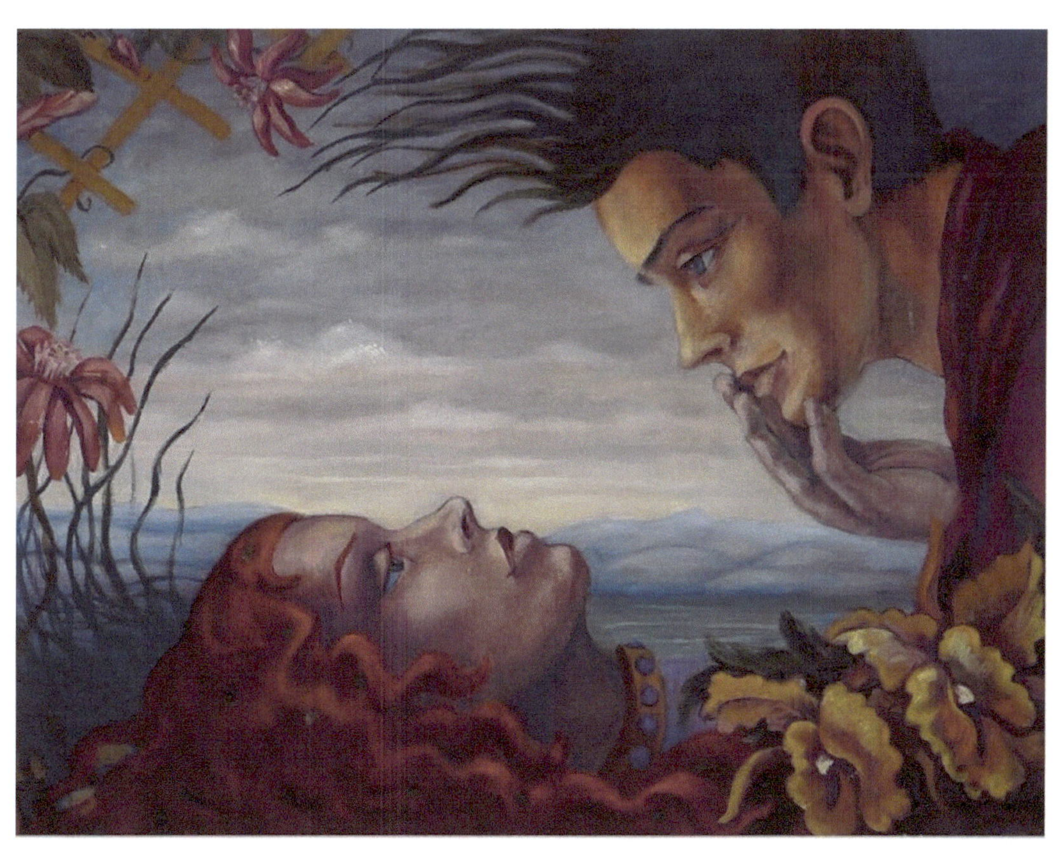

This painting depicts an ideal romantic relationship between a man and a woman. There is a surreal, dreamlike quality to the painting with the smoothly flowing hair, intertwining grass, and flowers in a circular motion. This circular motion represents the natural flow in the relationship when things work together easily and without forced effort. The shape of the grass and flowers is organic and sensual. These flowers emanate vibrantly the natural chemistry and sexual attraction between the man and woman. There is a gate around the flowers constraining them, but still, the beauty and sensuality of the flowers breaks through.

The woman's darker skin tone reflects that she is of the earth, emerging from it. Her position in the painting is like Gaia, the Greek ancestral Mother Earth. The man's green hair mirrors the green grass, reflecting the organic nature of sexual attraction and fertility. Attraction is part of nature. The man is like a traditional Green Man, a pagan symbol of fertility and rebirth.

The man came into her world from the sky, an unknown place, inexplicably and perfectly. Although they are surrounded by turbulent clouds, the couple is protected in their own world. Nothing touches them. The external environment at an unknown distance from them isn't warm or nurturing, but their connection is a personal paradise of their own creation.

The yellow collar with purple jewels represents the traditional social restraints placed upon the woman. Yellow represents social control, and purple represents traditional religious ideals and morality. The woman is restrained. The man is not. The collar represents the choices the woman was forced to make based on the constraints of society.

Despite the social traditions and sensibilities that the woman is bound by, love is an organic element that comes naturally to her through the cycle of nature that elevates her.

Love is depicted as a cyclical, organic connection between individuals that comes naturally as a part of life. Their love is something greater than this world. The warmth, compassion, and connection of their embrace contrasts with the coldness and starkness of the world outside.

This painting depicts an idealized dream of love that not everyone experiences in life. It's hopeful despite the constraints that are depicted everywhere. The only place without constraint is between the lovers. Feelings of love, tenderness, acceptance, and connection emanate from and between this very attractive couple.

Love Entwined

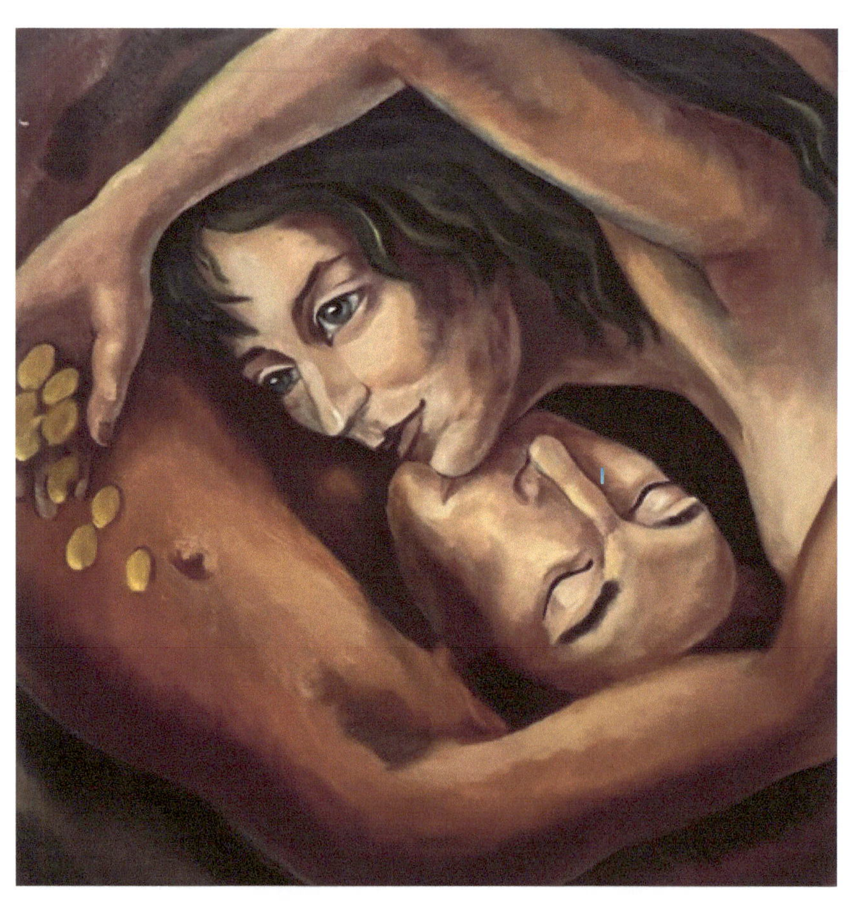

At first glance, this painting evokes a literal yin-yang. A man and woman are encircled in an infinite embrace floating through eternity.

The woman's green hair represents money. Money was always important to this woman, a cause of worry due to financial struggles. But in finding true love, the woman can let go of her financial fears, as represented in the golden coins falling from her hands. The man being embraced isn't focused on material status or seeking wealth. The lover's connection is based on deep, instinctual communication. The structure of the lover's embrace forms a circle, which reflects the transformative cycle of love that has changed the woman's perspective on life. The woman was under the control of money and social status at the beginning of the cycle. The woman let go of this fixation on money and status through her connection with real love. The lovers are in sync spiritually, rather than having money, with the financial and social status they bring, as the foundation of their relationship.

There is no pressure of social expectations in this relationship. After her transformation, the woman's green hair and eyes represent fertility and abundance, like a mythical Green Woman. The gold objects could be pieces of grain, fertilizing the world through the natural cycle of love. The woman lets go of what is superficial, materialistic, and unimportant to find true love on a deeper level. The reddish-brown background colors symbolize the darkness she's moving out of into the green of the lower left corner in the painting. The green represents the regenerative energy of love from the lovers that cycles through life.

❦

The Circus Series

The Circus Paintings were painted at a time of transition in Jana's life. She spent time in both Florida and Prague for a portion of the year. Moving from one world to another was both stressful and exciting. As a young woman, Jana idealized circuses, always wanting to run away and join one. These paintings are visually beautiful but have dark, repressive undertones. The bright colors give a feeling of joy. A closer look reveals a darker, restrictive emotional reality. The circus represents the social situation, the corresponding social roles, limitations, and pressures of a particular place that had to be adapted to.

The Circus Ring

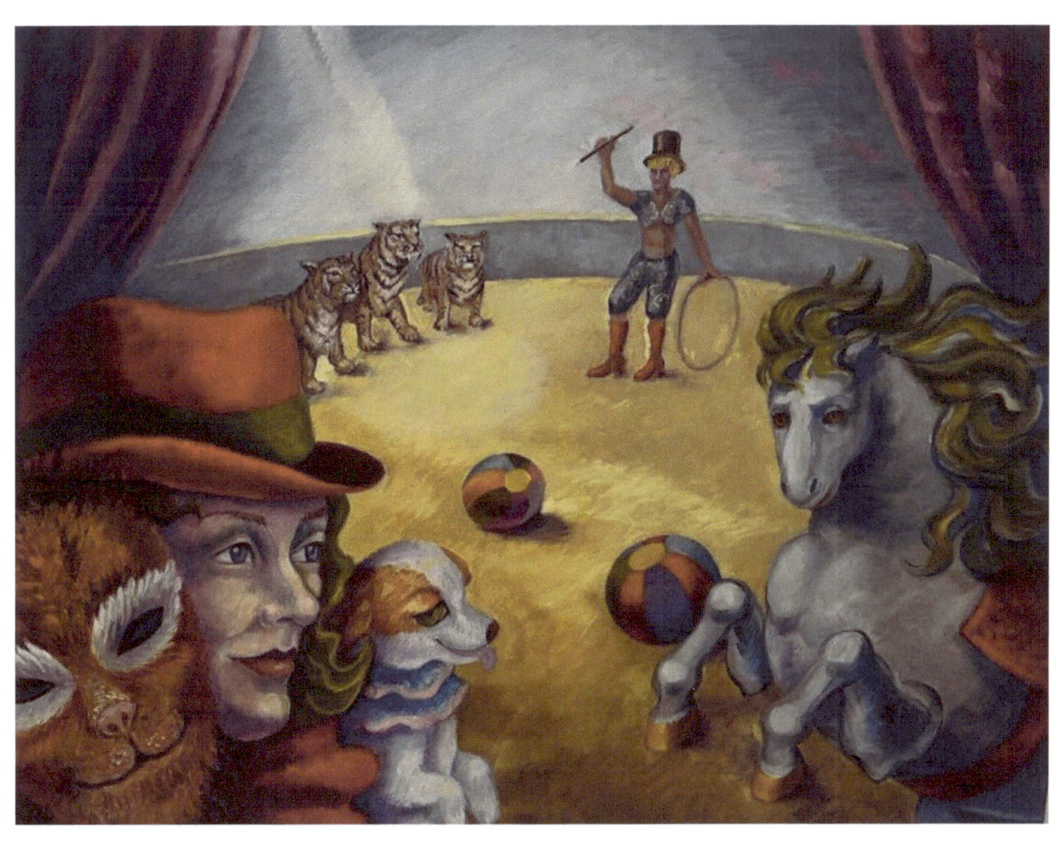

The circus scene in this painting is superficially joyful and lighthearted, but there are darker elements pulsing underneath the fun activities and bright colors. The circus has a female ringmaster holding a whip with three subdued tigers, a restrained horse, and a joker watching over everything. The female ringmaster is wearing a sexy halter top and boots with blue velvety short costume pants. The tigers must jump through the hoop. It's as if the female ringmaster must suppress her true powerful animal nature, represented by the three tigers, by conforming to social expectations about her role as a woman in the circus of life.

The horse wants to bolt but, like the other animals, is in a closed environment. The joker has a sinister smile and dark knowing eyes. The joker's dog is the most joyful animal in the circus. The dog symbolizes the superficially friendly and harmless social mask some people wear. There is also an imaginary cat-dog creature behind the joker. This animal represents the dark, predatory impulses that motivate the joker behind his friendly, attractive exterior. The purple curtains surround the superficial, typical circus activities on display. But the fear in the horse's eyes, the timidity of the tigers under the controlling whip of the ringmaster, and the mocking smile of the joker are disturbing. The audience is invisible behind a gray background.

The ringmaster keeps the animals under control. The circus seems joyful and full of fun and excitement externally, but there is a sinister, sad repression at a deeper level. The joker is watching and approves of the situation. The horse hasn't been broken like the tigers. Its green mane suggests strength and a connection to its true wild nature. The horse symbolizes the natural spirit that isn't controlled or broken by the social norms represented by the circus. The tigers, by contrast, aren't free and their spirits are broken. The tigers will never be able to explore their own true, wild nature. The horse will move beyond its fear to explore life and the new possibilities in the world once it escapes from the ring.

The horse represents the indomitable spirit that is true to itself. It isn't controlled by the rigidity and predictability of life in the circus. The circus represents the circumstances in life that are being broken through as change occurs. Life outside of the confined circus ring is unpredictable and unlimited. The joker watching everything from the left side embodies the social pressure that limits and controls the ring. The sense of conformity inside the ring is stifling and limiting. Despite the superficially joyful exterior, the deeper darker elements show the social constriction and repression from which Jana, like the horse, sought to escape.

The Circus Painting 2

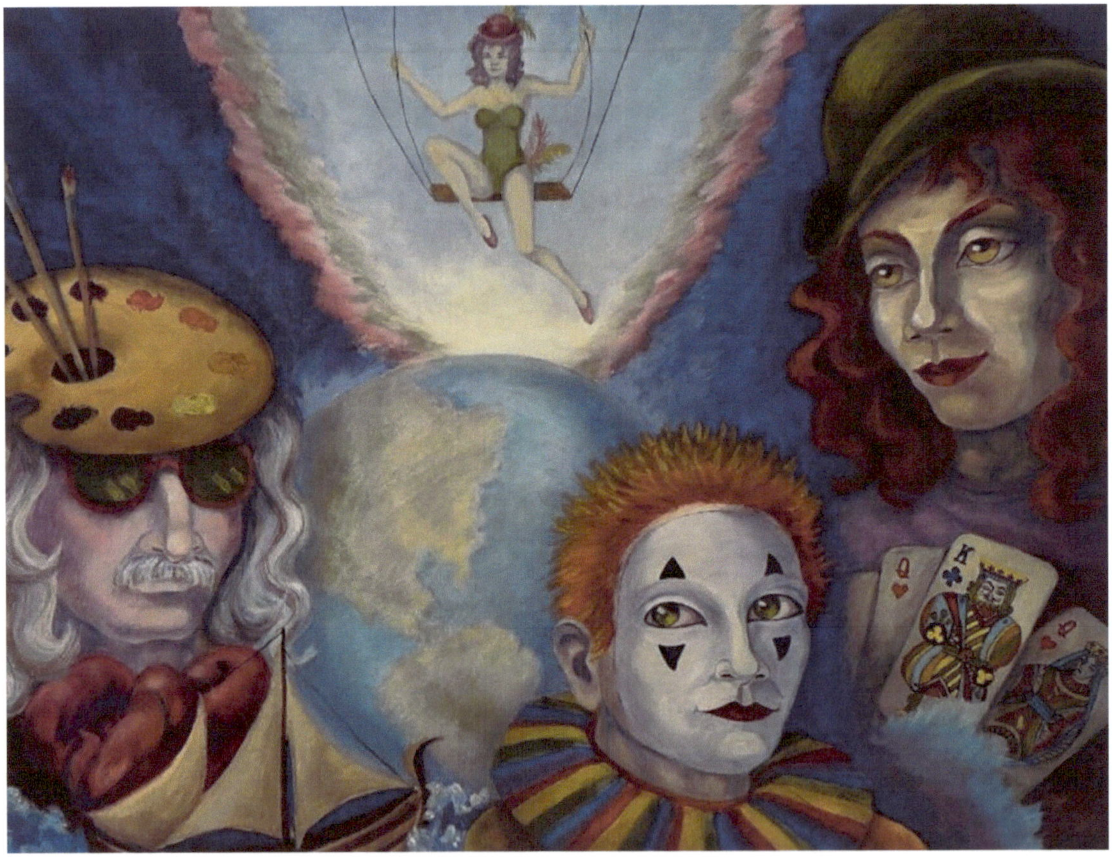

The painting depicts an around-the-world experience as well as Jana's transition and adaptation to her new circumstances.

The earth is centered behind a sailboat, navigating rough tides. The circus performers travel around the world. The female trapeze artist is swinging between two different parts of the world. Neither world is her home completely. The bright light behind the trapeze artist darkens as she swings forward into the night sky, moving from the known into the unknown.

The globe at the center signifies Jana's movement around from one world to another. Jana spent part of the year in Prague and part of the year in Miami at the time this painting was created. It reflects the difficulties in Jana's transition and adaptation to her new circumstances. The chaos of moving back and forth is reflected in the surrealistic elements of the painting.

The card motif reappears in this painting with the king of clubs and two queens of hearts, one by the king's side and the other queen of hearts hidden behind the king. The king is confident and masculine, while the visible queen of hearts is more withdrawn. The king's eyes are closed to the queen's pain. The unseen queen of hearts behind the king suggests infidelity and mistrust.

The circus people represent different elements in the new life that the trapeze artist is swinging into.

The orange haired clown is physically fit and striking with piercing green eyes that are slightly bloodshot. His position at the front of the painting suggests control and leadership. The clown is entertaining and unpredictable but also serious and forceful. He directs the movement.

The older, longer-haired artist with green sunglasses views the world through an artistic lens. The artist's hat is a paint pallet with brushes poking out of his head, signifying that art is how he processes the world.

The young red-haired woman wearing a green bowler hat is sympathetic and grounded. She is androgynous and physically fit. She's wearing the same colors as the trapeze artist. Her presence is comforting and loving, with eyes that depict a knowledge of suffering and difficulties in their world.

The Circus 3

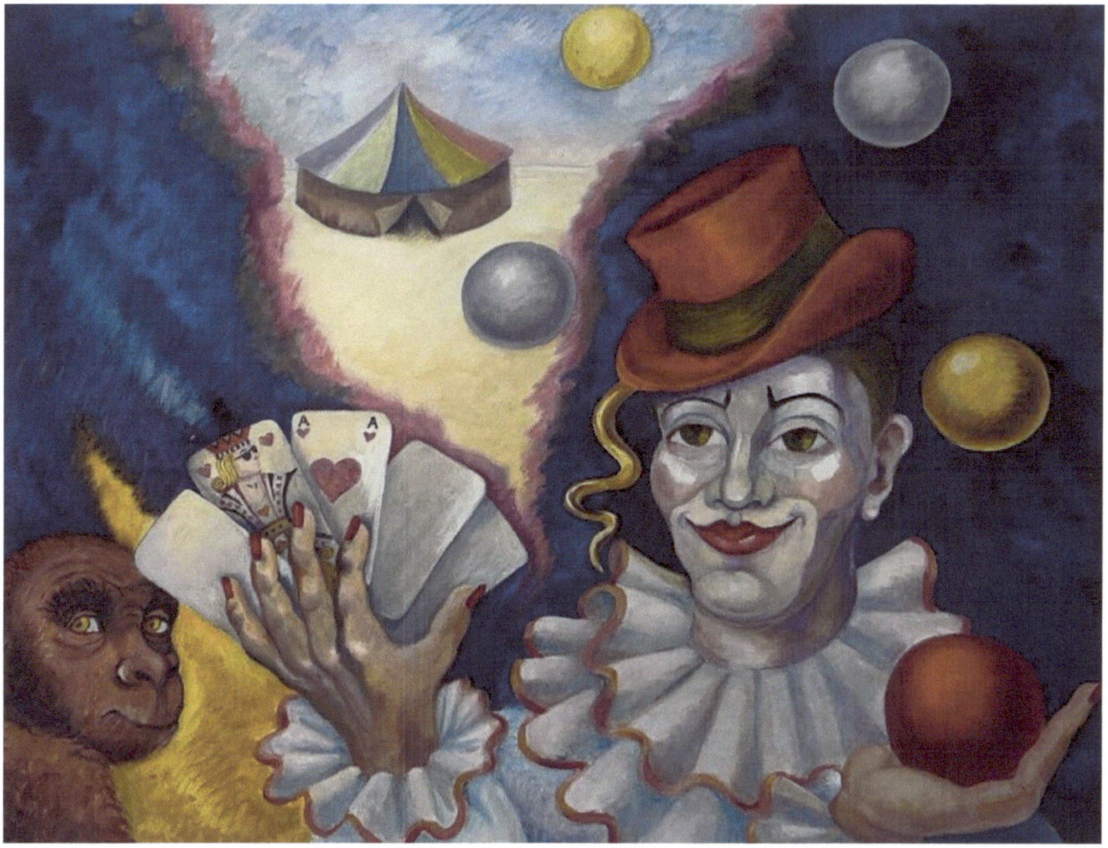

The clown at the center of this painting is juggling many balls and has a deck of cards. He's attractive but enigmatic and hard to discern. Can he be trusted or not? The clown is enveloped in the activity but somehow also detached from it. His smile is bright and sensual, emphasized by his bright orange hat with a green ribbon. There is a sense that the clown is trying to take advantage of someone with illusions and tricks.

The clown is holding the king of hearts card with the ace of hearts behind it. The king of hearts has sunglasses on, blinded to the suffering of others and enveloped in his own image and self-importance. The king gets love and attention for presenting the correct social image in the circus of life. The King doesn't have an equal partner, just a depersonalized source of love. The other cards are blank, showing that the king doesn't have anything else but his narcissistic sense of self-importance, which is validated by society.

The monkey-gorilla creature in the left corner expresses an instinctual wisdom and understanding that is unadorned and raw. This creature sees a deeper truth behind the colorful clown's makeup and flashy tricks. This animal is thinking about how to survive and isn't concerned with external appearances. The monkey-gorilla isn't caged or constricted by social norms. The clown seeks to use social norms to control and manipulate.

The monkey-gorilla and the clown represent two opposing forces. The clown is superficial, manipulative, and untrustworthy. The monkey-gorilla is natural, kind, and instinctual. The animal is authentic and wise. The monkey-gorilla can navigate difficulties and see beyond superficiality to survive. Everyone is playing their role in the circus of life.

The scene behind the two figures is a circus tent, representing the society and world left behind. This painting represents the movement from one circus to another circus with these figures representing the process, and different people and situations encountered along the way. The joker, appearing to be more modern, has a cold stare and an unknown agenda hidden behind his mask.

$\mathcal{S}$

Political Paintings

The paintings in this section reflect on post-communist politics, the possibility of war, an ultimate sense of detachment, and looking beyond.

Nude Woman on a Table

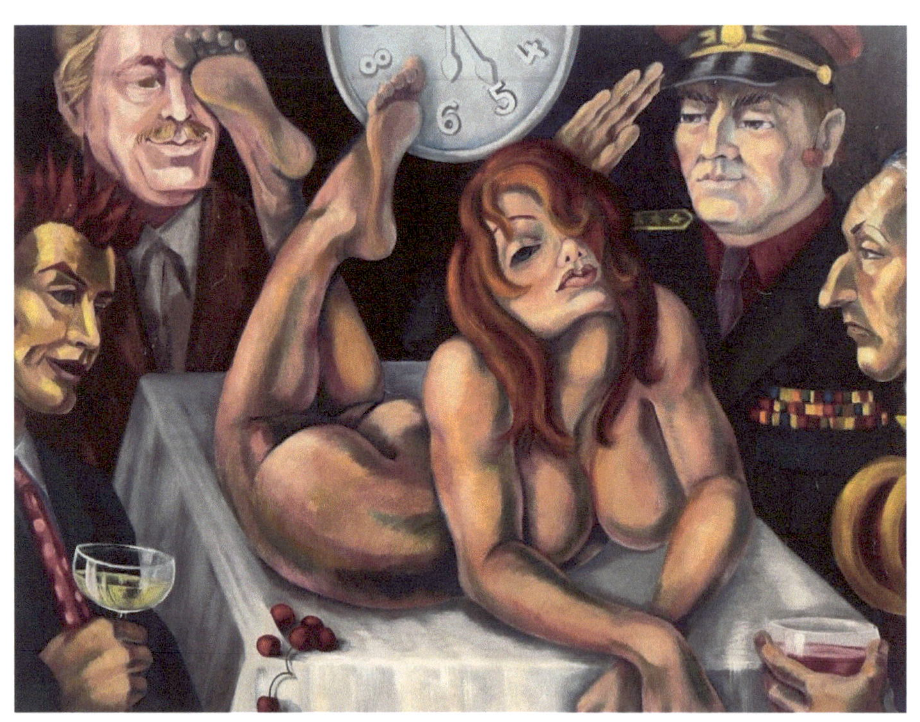

This painting depicts a nude woman in the middle of a table surrounded by Vaclav Havel, the late former President of the Czech Republic, other men, and military leaders. The voluptuous woman, the only unclothed figure, is being served up as the center of an orgiastic feast that the clothed men presumably will fight over. The woman represents not only feminine freedom, but the freedom of Czech people in general. The nude woman's contrast with the clothed male military figures show the repression and male-dominated control that still exists, even after the fall of communism. The communistic repression of women still runs through Czech society with the new democratic president.

The only identifiable male figure is the simply dressed Vaclav Havel who is depicted as a new leader, surrounded by the old political system that he doesn't completely see or understand. All of them have blank stares, while Havel has no eyes at all. The woman is completely objectified, with no innate value to any of the men. She is natural but only fulfills their sexual desires.

The bottom of the clock represents the timelessness of these attitudes towards women. Despite the new generation of leaders in the Czech Republic, some things never change. The leadership is blind to women in any other kind of role.

Jana painted this after returning to the newly formed Czech Republic when Havel was president after the Velvet Revolution. Just as when she lived there before, young and beautiful women get attention and are desired until they become older babushkas. Then they fade from influence and social importance.

The woman represents the Czech Republic itself surrounded by fighting political factions hoping to carve it up or possess it for themselves. She is being fought over and possibly sold off to the highest bidder.

Although Havel, a playwright, was a good, kind person, he wasn't viewed by many Czechs as being strong enough to rule the country effectively. Havel is represented as pale and studious, as opposed to the uncomplicated tanned and toned nude woman. The communist military leaders are pale, austere and cold, reflecting their lack of compassion and humanity in taking away people's freedom and happiness. The elderly gentleman surrounding the table represents the old political guard holding on.

There is a sense of mistrust towards the whole political system, even after the end of communism. Havel was from the middle class. This was a departure from the political leadership as usually politicians were born into wealth and position. A romantic figure, he gave the Czech people hope that an average person could become president and help the general population, outside of the ruling class. But he was not an experienced politician and struggled to work within the new system of government, which still had the vestiges of communism. The end of communism ushered in a period of tremendous change, with many new immigrants coming into the country buying up property and businesses from Czechs who needed the money. Corruption set in, but with an element of hope for the newly democratic form of government and its noble, well-meaning president.

The Road to War

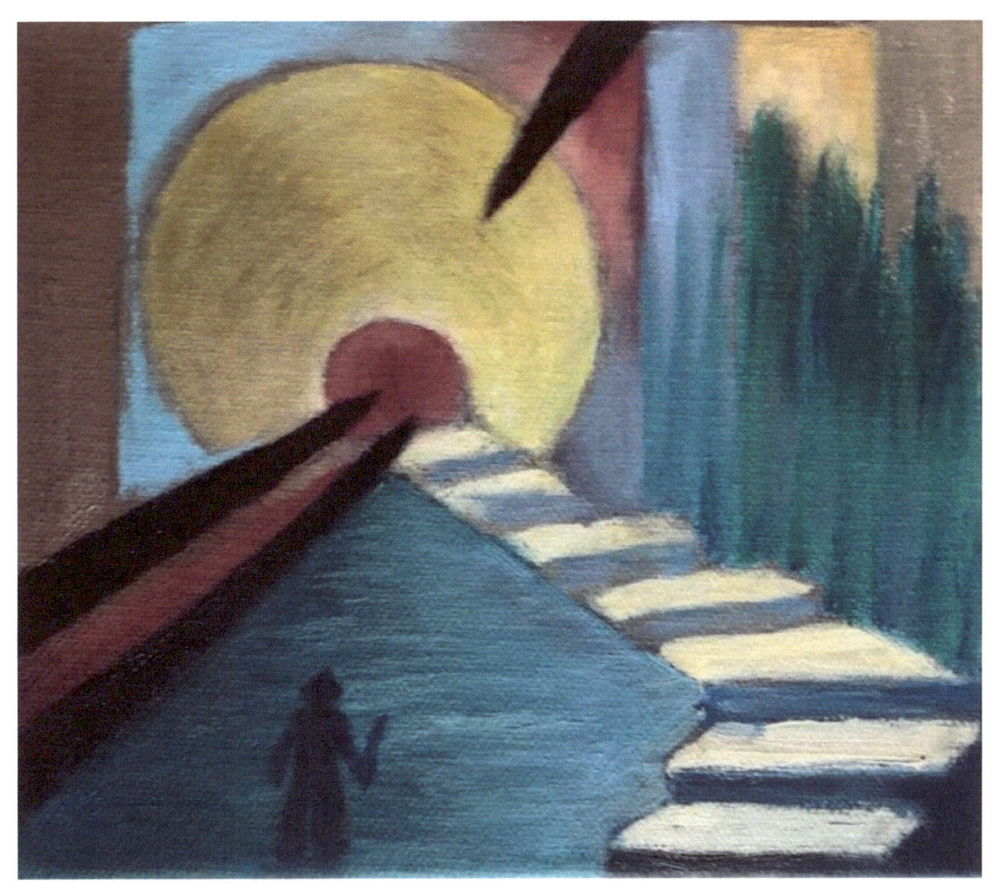

This painting, from 2023, differs greatly in style and subject matter from Jana's other paintings. Other than the colors and certain structural elements, the painting looks completely different than Jana's other works. The images aren't as clear or precise as her other paintings where the lines and outlines are very distinct. There is a more rugged feeling to this painting. She frequently paints subject matter that is stressful or upsetting to her on some level. It's as if she is processing these feelings through the painting to obtain an emotional resolution and feel more at peace.

The painting depicts a path through a tunnel with some light. The jagged, sharp, piercing lines are like swords, trying to reach the center of the tunnel. The person heading towards that tunnel is uncharacteristically non-descript, representing anybody or everybody. The lines could be metal objects, representing instruments of war reminiscent of medieval times. There is a sense of uncertainty as the war may or may not affect this person. The red at the end of the lit tunnel represents fire, war, fear, and blood. Images of nuclear bombs and weapons of war retaliating against each other loom at the end of the blood path to destruction.

Is the normal path of life turning into a path to death and destruction?

There is a hopeful element, depicted in the pathway alongside the woods. The every-man figure can choose to walk into the forest instead of continuing on the path to war through the tunnel. She uses arches, a common element in many of her architectural paintings depicting Prague, to create a framework for war. Although war seems far away, is the path to war inevitable, or is there another option?

The frame in the painting is a painted frame towards the top only. The lack of frame at the bottom of the painting represents openness and uncertainty, as if society is trying to hold things together in a frame, but there is uncertainty as to whether or not that social framework will hold. Society is trying to keep things boxed in and predictable, but that's not possible.

There are more abstract shapes within the clarity of the frame and steps. This is another departure from Jana's previous style. The future is unclear and frightening. The forest represents a hopeful element. Life and nature will go on no matter what.

The every-man figure has a choice. Are they going to continue down the path to war, or will they choose the path to life? It's a crossroads. The person isn't on the path yet and could end up in a beautiful place or in war. The every-man figure doesn't know which direction they will take yet. Will they choose peace in the forest or the path to war? The fact that the person isn't on the path yet is a hopeful sign. It's not inevitable quite yet. Maybe there's a choice and maybe there isn't a choice. It's wherever the path takes society.

At the time Jana painted this, the idea of war was looming, always in the back of everyone's mind in Prague. She knows war all too well, having been born in 1940 during the Nazi occupation of World War II, and then experiencing the Cold War and Russian occupation not long after. This painting represents European anxiety and fear about impending war, a collective memory they don't want to repeat.

The Road Above

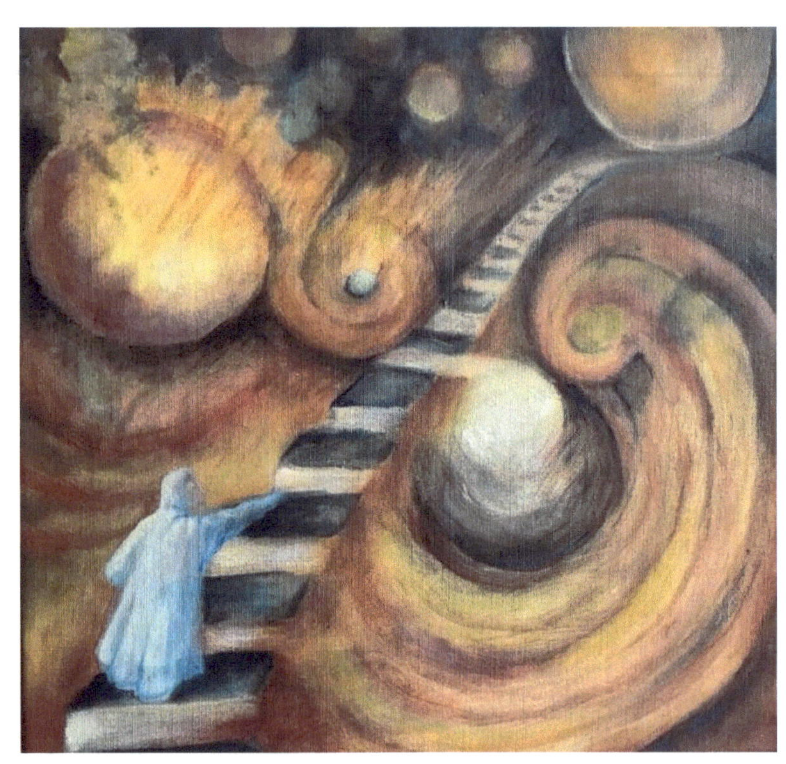

This painting reflects Jana's shift into abstraction. It's not a complete shift, as there are still recognizable forms moving into and around abstract images. The pathway depicted at the center is reminiscent of the pathway in other paintings by Jana from this period. The pathway is taking her into an abstract universe, as if she is looking into the world beyond this lifetime.

On one level, the lone figure is surrounded by fire and explosions and stays on the path, detached from it. The fiery explosions are also cyclical and organic, representing the ebb and flow of life that is constantly changing. Jana has lived in many different worlds in her lifetime, but somehow has managed to forge her way through them on a singular artistic path.

The ball of life at the end is hopeful. The many organic circles represent the children she brought to life and possible paths that could have been taken but weren't. One cyclical wave could represent her older daughter on her own pathway, while the filled circle could represent a full womb and her younger daughter who has remained physically close to her. The ball of light intersecting the path is indicative of Jana processing the light and darkness in her life in a reflective way. There are many worlds spinning around the lone figure on the path through turmoil, who proceeds ahead without fear.

The circles depicted in the explosion take on the form of the human body in an almost cubist way. The circle in the upper left corner looks like a female breast while another looks like an eyeball. Another form is indicative of human ribs. It's as if the universe is a giant womb, giving birth to all life in fiery passion, like the Great Goddess.

This painting reflects a new cycle of life for Jana. The energies around her previously depicted in forms are now shown at a purely energetic level, where she is the only form depicted.

The loss of her life partner unexpectedly led Jana to think about what comes after this life and how that world is. Her marriage was filled with unexpected turmoil, adventure, and world travel.

The path of the person is above the earth with the planets exploding below her, not affecting her or her trajectory forward. The universe is the giant mother, and the traveler is returning to her. The universe is a womb, containing Jana's life and the people she's cyclically connected to and whom she still nurtures. It's an energetic map of the cycles in her life that swirl and explode around her as she moves towards another world.

Nature

Jana's sunflowers and birds reflect her reverence for the animals and lush greenery by her two homes in Prague and Miami Beach. The animals mirror human behavior and dynamics.

Sunflowers

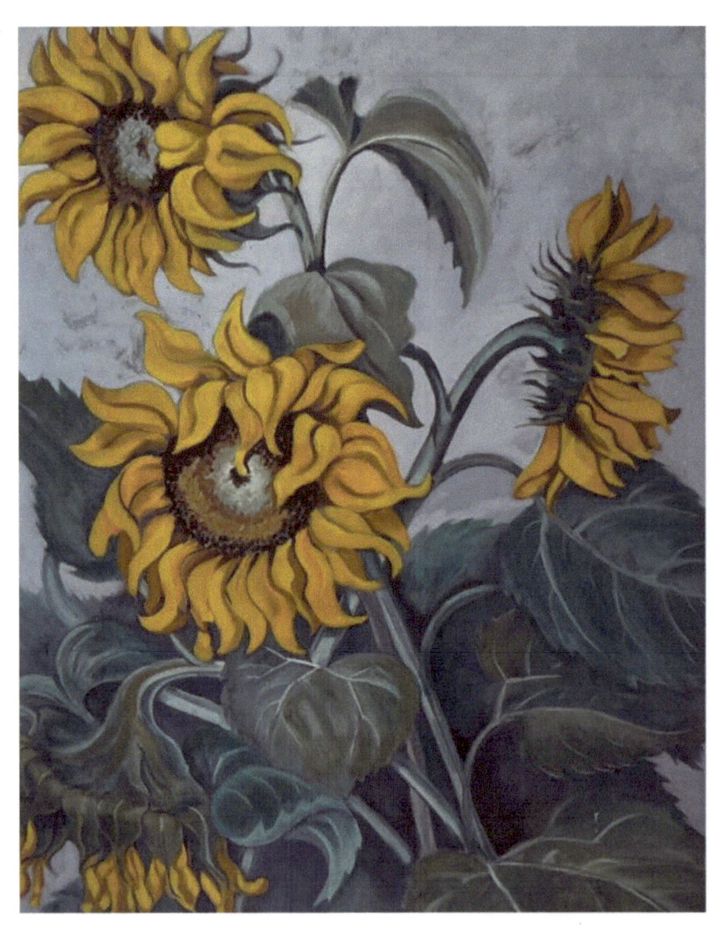

Sunflowers fill the fields of the Czech countryside surrounding the cottage of Jana's late in-laws. She and her two daughters spent many afternoons sitting and playing in these fields that served as the inspiration for this painting. Jana painted the sunflowers after a teenage Claudia pleaded with her to memorialize her favorite flower.

Jana, her husband, and daughters visited the Czech Republic during communism when it was allowed. This painting was done during that period. She had to paint quickly because sunflowers wilt in a short time.

The original sunflower painting was stolen. Jana's mother-in-law wanted another sunflower painting. She and her father-in-law searched the gardens around their cottage to find sunflowers as models. Eventually, after much effort, they found sunflowers in an abandoned garden. She painted non-stop for three days to complete it.

Although Jana paints flowers "as they are" in nature, she enhanced their colors to make them more brilliant and expressive. These flowers, sometimes beautiful, sometimes wounded, sometimes wild or perfectly aligned, were painted as they grow in nature, not as stylistically perfect.

Following the life cycle in nature, sunflowers start off energetic and strong, growing to a towering size before ageing and withering. But even as they wither, there is maturity and beauty, reflective of the wisdom gained through surviving life's experiences over time.

Sunflowers, larger than most other flowers, are resilient, always finding a way to grow through vegetation however thick or rambled, to get to the sun.

Two of the flowers seem to peer out of the canvas like eyes watching the viewer in an all-knowing way. The viewer is looking at the flower and the flower is looking at the viewer, like the "Mona Lisa" effect of nature. The juxtaposition of the flowers themselves reflects the cycle of life. There are flowers at different levels. The flower at the top is at its peak. The two flowers in the middle level are drifting, while the flower at the bottom is withering.

Birds of a Feather

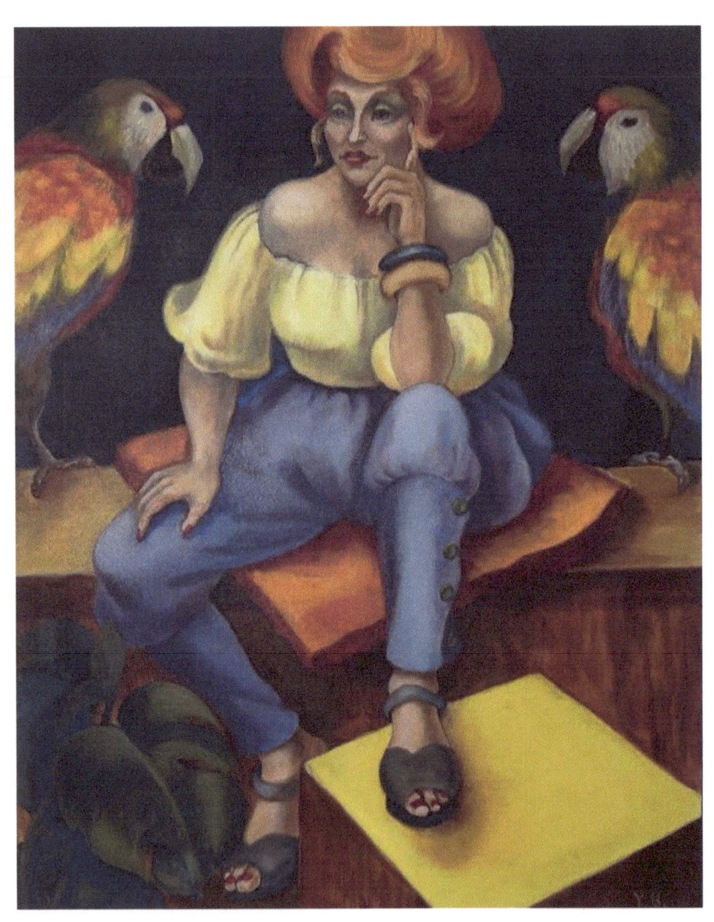

The woman depicted in this painting is judgmental, with a cold detachment, looking at everything without being a part of it. Criticism comes easily to her. She criticizes the things and people around her.

The two parrots on either side of the woman mirror and reflect this same critical attitude. There is a feeling of discontent and disharmony. Everything in this woman's life must be precise. The yellow and purple bracelets matching her yellow shirt and purple pants represent control, and suggest a regal presence, and a traditional, controlled sense of spirituality. She is probably a church lady. The red, representing grounding in the physical world, and orange, representing sensuality, show that she is living in her lower, physical nature. Projecting the perfect image, with her painted nails and flawless hairstyle, is what motivates this woman. She is focused on physical reality and perfection, not on intellect or compassion. She has the capacity for humanity, as reflected in her eyes, but she's an artificial person.

One foot is on the yellow tile, suggesting that the woman is partially grounded in everyday life and could stop focusing on a false ideal of perfection and toxic criticism and judgment if she wanted to. The other foot off the ground represents that she's not completely grounded in reality because of her false expectations of perfection for herself and others. The woman is the only one who can make that decision. She can choose to follow the path in front of her, filled with foliage and greenery, representing a life of freedom and life as it is without judgment. But even the plants themselves are regimented indoor plants that need to be dusted and polished. The plants are beautiful and controlled, like the woman herself.

Everything about this woman represents discontent. Although she's surrounded by the colorful birds and lush plants, the woman doesn't see them. She is looking beyond to an empty world that is shining and beautiful, but ultimately not real or satisfying. The woman herself is like a colorful bird, cackling and gossipy, attracting other women like her. This woman is the perfect image of what society expects her to be, and she has complied.

There is a more human side to her, but the superficial side of control and perfection is what dominates. She is socially acceptable, but it comes at a cost. She conforms to society with the perfect image, but it comes at the cost of her humanity. She mirrors the colors of the birds, as if she herself is the kind of colorful bird society expects her to be. She is like a parrot—colorful, gossipy, superficial, and admired by society. Her inflexibility traps the woman in a world that only she can control by projecting the perfect image.

This woman is the complete antithesis of Jana Bemová. Many times, she paints the opposite of what she thinks or values as a way of processing and releasing aspects of life that are constraining or distressing.

Jana's life was filled with women like this. Many of her paintings depict these kinds of socially acceptable women, reflecting the pressure she felt growing up in a traditional European social structure within which she felt constrained, controlled, and limited. She resisted and fought back against these social expectations and the direct and overwhelming need for social perfection, refusing to conform.

Birds of Paradise

This series of paintings was painted while Jana lived in Miami Beach. After a hurricane, many tropical birds escaped from their enclosures and were flying through the trees. Impossible to ignore because of their noisy squawking, these birds nestled in the palm trees and tropical vegetation around the bay. She observed these birds on her daily walks around the small island on Miami Beach where they lived. Although these birds are an accurate representation of natural colorful beauty, the movement and juxtaposition of the birds reflect the real human dynamics that Jana observed. She found sanctuary being in nature, free from social restrictions, expectations, and pressures.

Two Parrots on a Limb

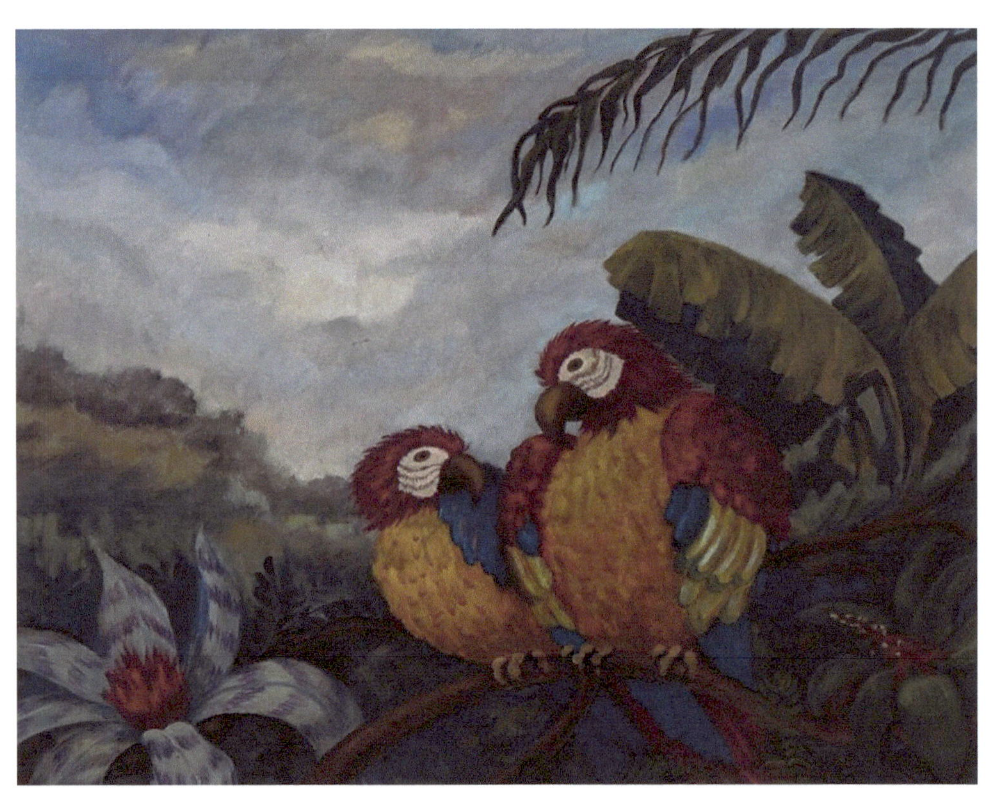

This painting depicts two parrots perched on a tree limb. The larger bird is dominant over the smaller, passive bird. Their orange plumage in the center reflects their intimate connection. The yellow feathers on the edge of the larger parrot's wings show that he controls the movement, while the submissive bird waits for his command.

They are perched on a branch surrounded by lush greenery, but the churning clouds behind the birds suggest a possible storm bringing unknown turmoil and destruction.

Three Parrots

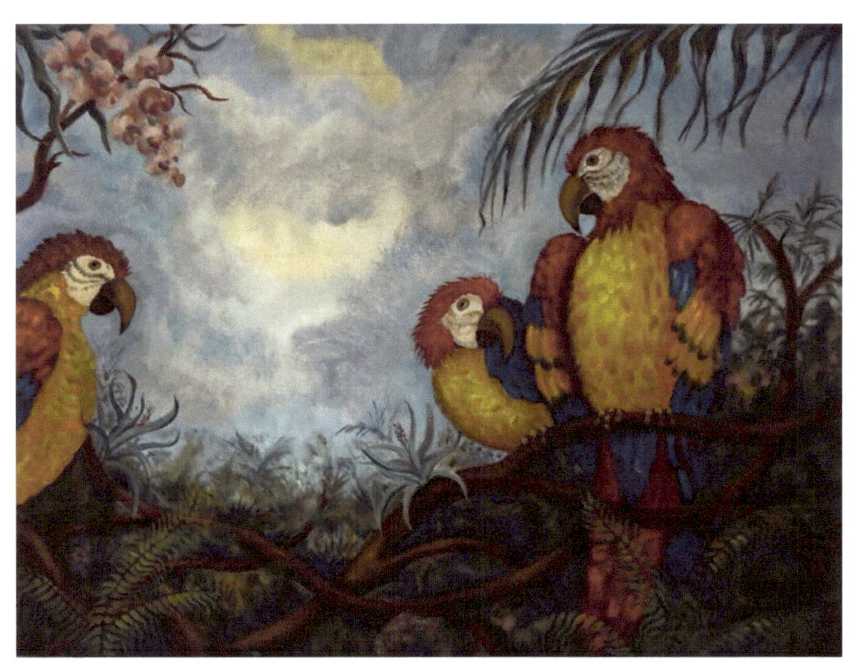

This same parrot couple from "Two Parrots on a Limb" is depicted with their offspring. The dominant male bird is looking down judgmentally at the young bird, who is cowering under his disapproving gaze. The mother bird is watching this dynamic from another branch, unable to change anything between them. It's as if the mother bird is watching the problems of, and between, the baby bird and the father bird.

There is a feeling of concern as to what will happen next to the members of this nest. The clouds in the background form a frightened and confused woman's face, which could also be a tunnel going to somewhere unknown through the clouds. The clouds almost form a mini tornado, as if conflict and destruction are in the not-so-distant future.

Two Parrots on a Limb with One Taking Flight

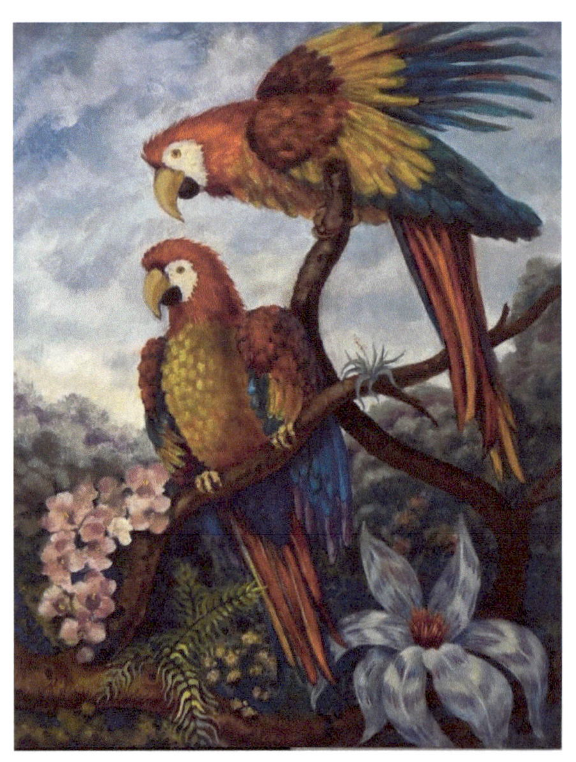

The vibrant colors of these two parrots express the strength, resilience, joy, and comfort of living in their lush tropical paradise, free in the natural environment. They are almost the same size, representing their equality and mutual support. These symbiotic birds are gazing in the same direction harmoniously. The seated parrot is watching her younger companion launch herself off the tree limb and into a joyful adventure. There is movement in the parrot's wings and in the clouds behind them. It's as if the parrot's flight is lifting the dark clouds, brightening the darkness behind them.

Four Parrots on a Limb

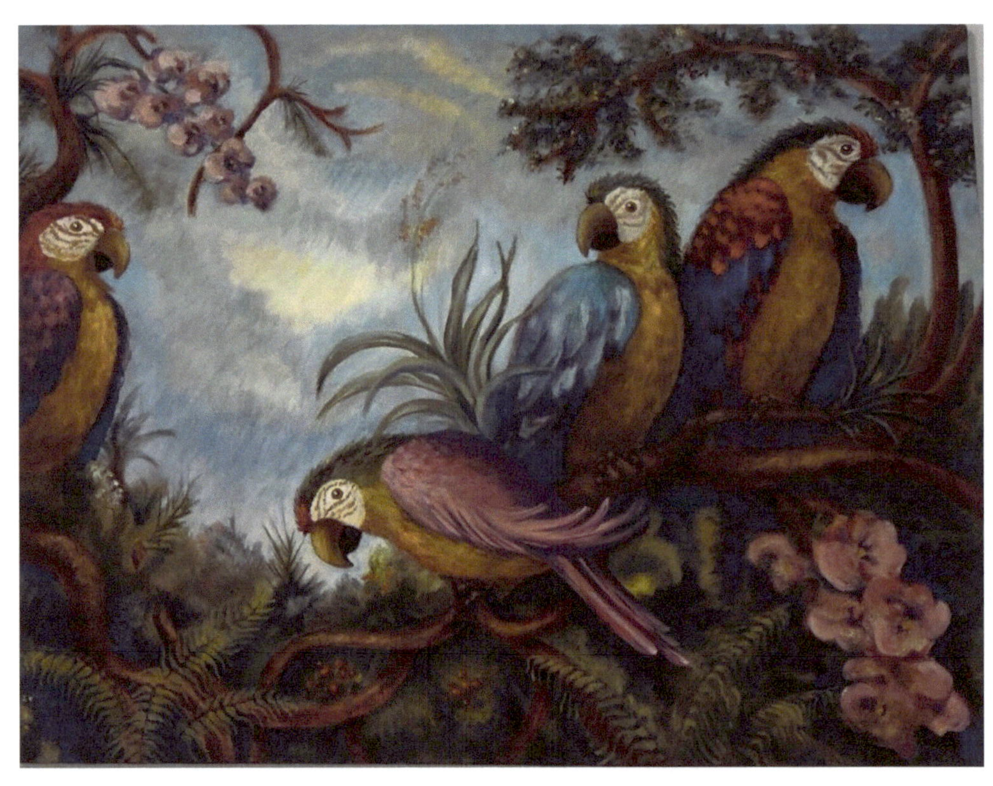

These parrots are multicolored, much like the previous parrots. Jana has imposed her own colorful imaginary pallet on these usually green parrots. In contrast to the softness of their pastel colors and the tropical lushness of the greenery around them, this painting depicts the tension, isolation, and conflict between these colorful creatures. None of the parrots are looking at each other. The small, pink-winged parrot is shamefully singled out and separated, looking down at the ground below.

The larger dominant parrot on the far-right side is looking away in disgust, perhaps influenced by the medium blue-winged parrot to his left. The blue-winged parrot is looking coldly and judgmentally at the small pink-winged parrot cowering. The purple-winged parrot is detached on a nearby limb, watching and unable to influence the dynamics between the other birds. It's as if they are pushing the small pink-winged parrot out of the nest and family group.

The clouds in the sky are swirling, forming a tornado-like tunnel that could envelop the small parrot into an unknown and dangerous world. This painful emotional dynamic is contrasted with the colorful beauty of these birds in their lavish, tropical environment.

The Toucan

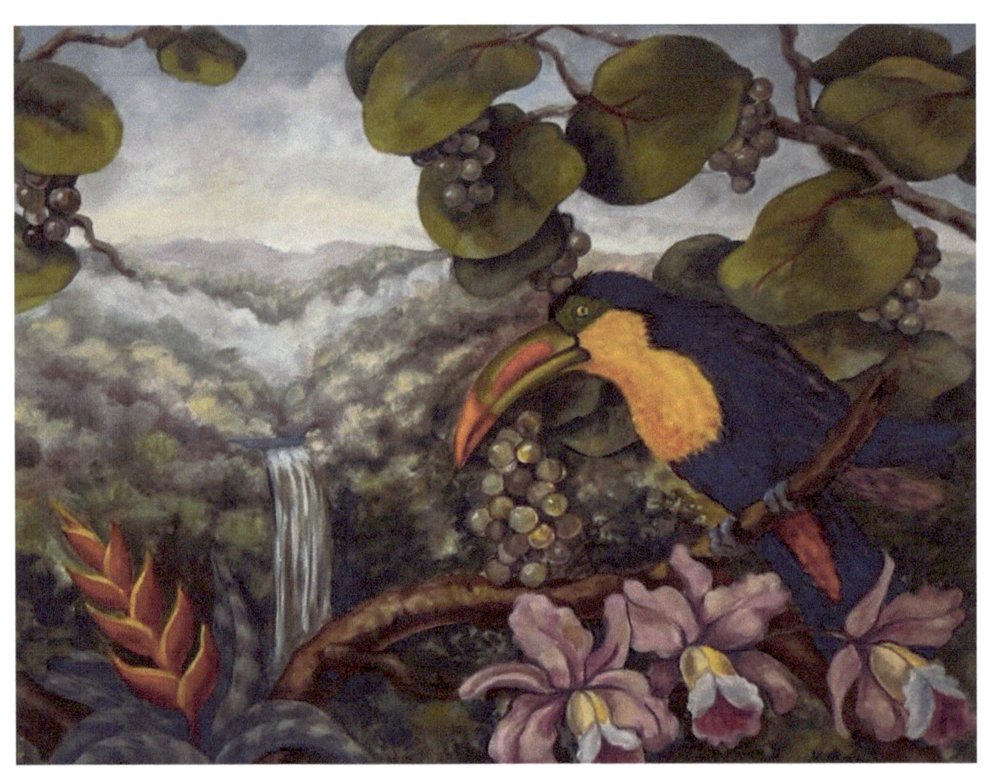

The toucan is solitary, enveloped in the beauty around it. The bird is peacefully unified with nature, without conflict in its own space. There is abundance and richness in the flowers, trees, and leaves. There are grapes to eat and an endless supply of water to drink from the waterfall.

This toucan represents Jana as an artist. The waterfall represents the wellspring of inspiration that she finds from being in nature. The environment feeds her with its beauty. Her creative ideas develop and grow naturally, like flowers blooming. The imaginary flower with blue striped leaves is present in two of the previous parrot paintings but has completed its fiery growth with the toucan.

Jana gave birth to these bird paintings by observing the natural world around her in a solitary way, blending into the beauty, and creating her own world in which to inhabit and express herself as an artist.

Jana Bemová and Claudia Zoeller

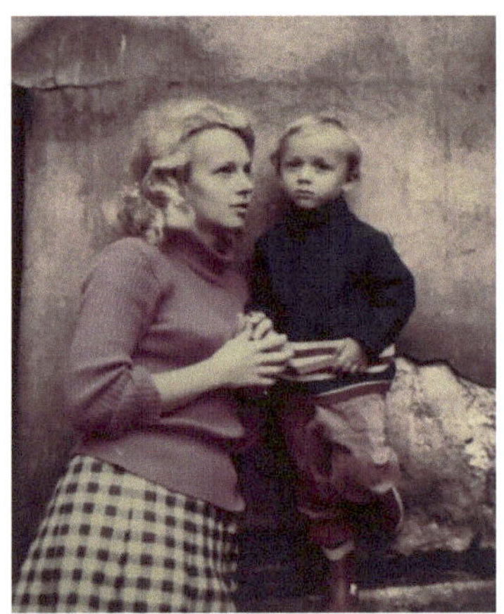

This book is a biography of the artist Jana Bemová as expressed through her paintings thematically. It focuses on seminal events in the artist's life and how these circumstances were processed and reflected in her paintings.

Acknowledgements

With special thanks to Roberto Scimonelli for his contributions to the book.

Additional thanks to Leonardo Scimonelli for editing.

In memory of John Zoeller, Karel Ulrich, and Vera Ulrichová.

This book was written based on interviews with Jana Bemová and her eldest daughter, Claudia Zoeller. Claudia's voice and interpretation resound through the text. Both she and her younger sister, Jan Marie, lived with their mother's paintings and observed her daily artistic process as they struggled through life's challenges. Jana's paintings are a narrative of their shared life together, a visual diary spanning her entire life. This book captures a small portion of the prolific number of paintings she has created, and those selected for inclusion in this book reflect the most important and impactful aspects of her life. This text interprets the personal, reflective, and transformative themes expressed in her paintings.

About the Authors

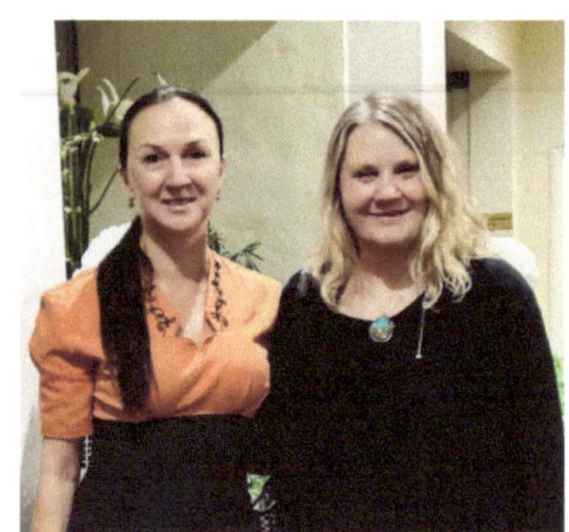

Claudia Zoeller (pictured left) is Jana Bemova's eldest daughter. She currently spends time between the US and Czechia. She works in the health and fitness field and manages a warehouse company in south Florida. When she's not teaching fitness classes, she enjoys traveling, outdoor activities, attending art openings, and discovering new cafés.

Joan Yesulaitis (pictured right) is a freelance writer and English teacher. She is fluent in English and Spanish and currently lives in Florida and North Carolina.